Acc. No. BK 28836 Class

MID CHESHIRE COLLEGE

HARTFORD, CHESHIRE

ORDER No. 7808

D1631824

**This book is to be returned on or before
the last date stamped below.**

27 FEB 1998	2 9 JAN 2003	
19 MAR 1998	-8 OCT 2003	
23 APR 1998	2 3 FEB 2004	
11 NOV 1998	-9 OCT 2009	
27 APR 2000	1 3 APR 2011	
13 APR 2000		
2 MAY 2000		
12 JAN 2001		
26 FEB 2002		
07 JAN 2003		LIBREX

BK28836

ARCHITECTURE
THE NEW MODERN

ARCHITECTURE
THE NEW MODERN

CARLA BREEZE

Architecture and Interior Design Library

AN IMPRINT OF
PBC INTERNATIONAL, INC.

Distributor to the book trade in the United States and Canada
Rizzoli International Publications Inc.
300 Park Avenue South
New York, NY 10010

Distributor to the art trade in the United States and Canada
PBC International, Inc.
One School Street
Glen Cove, NY 11542

Distributor throughout the rest of the world
Hearst Books International
1350 Avenue of the Americas
New York, NY 10019

Copyright © 1995 by
PBC International, Inc.
All rights reserved. No part of this book may be
reproduced in any form whatsoever without
written permission of the copyright owner,
PBC International, Inc.
One School Street, Glen Cove, NY 11542

Library of Congress Cataloging–in–Publication Data

Breeze, Carla

        Architecture: the new modern / by Carla Breeze.
           p.   cm.
        Includes bibliographical references and index.
        ISBN 0-86636-436-6
        1. Architecture, Domestic—United States 2. Architecture—
Modern—20th century—United States I. Title
NA7208.B74 1995   94–38699
728' .0973'09045—dc20   CIP

CAVEAT– Information in this text is believed accurate, and will pose no problem for
the student or casual reader. However, the author was often constrained by information
contained in signed release forms, information that could have been in error or not
included at all. Any misinformation (or lack of information) is the result of failure in
these attestations. The author has done whatever is possible to insure accuracy.

Color separation, printing and binding by Toppan Printing Co., H.K.

Design: Pamela Fogg

10 9 8 7 6 5 4 3 2 1

Printed in Hong Kong

To Marcus Whiffen, kind friend and mentor

CONTENTS

INTRODUCTION

A rampant Robocop mentality gives the concept of "home" today a special poignancy. Home is a haven from the barrage of violence, consumerism, and the chaos of urban space in the process of what British architects Christine Hawley and Peter Cook have termed "dynamic collapse." It may symbolize stability, security, and traditional values, or nurture individual visions—a personal utopia controlled by the inhabitant. Function and fantasy often share the same dwelling. Media sources allow us to conceive of our personal environments as stages—a French provincial farmhouse, a Tudor manor, or an amusing bricolage of New England vernacular and technology.

Residential architecture embodies a paradox. The architect has greater freedom to experiment with flow and penetration of spaces, materials, and intellectual concepts—elements that might pose unacceptable risk for a commercial venture. The clients, however, are impelled by other forces: stability and security. Reverence for the past, in the form of applied cornices, columns, and pediments, is pervasive, and may impede the architect's pure vision.

Stuffed teddy bears lashed to the radiator grilles of sanitation vehicles, to the fence of an urban garden, or protruding from urban dwellers' backpacks, express an atavistic attachment to warmth and love. Public display of these tendencies is not always so flamboyant. Usually, it is only within our domiciles that we can indulge in space as a reflection of our values. Subjected to an increasingly technocentric electronic and mechanical world, we turn to home as an antidote and refuge from an environment degraded by pollution, overuse, and lack of care. Postmodern complexity coexists with the human desire for intimacy, shared memories, and rituals. As the next millennium evolves, the paradox of residence as personal space, secure retreat, office, and global communications center is being resolved through design.

Contemporary perceptions are shaped by the onslaught of new technologies, from video telephones to nuclear time-pieces, while overpopulation and stressed-out environmental limits present the

opposite New and old are juxtaposed in architect Peter L. Gluck's Reflected Farmhouse, an Upstate New York project involving the construction of a new house linked to an existing 19th-century farmhouse. Traditional farm-building elements are reinterpreted in the new portions of the structure, such as the barrel-vaulted lap pool enclosure that is reminiscent of a horizontally situated silo.
photo Carla Breeze

above The somewhat sentimental attachment to "familiar" architectural forms is particularly strong within the realm of residential design, countering the technological overload of life in the late 1990s.
photo Carla Breeze

possibility that the physical world may be a parody of any dystopia imaginable. The original Modernist quest for order, rational design, the integration of industry and technology, and a social agenda culminated in two types of residential projects, the infrastructures of the individual house and multiple dwellings on a massive scale. Both forms provide for sanitation, the delivery of potable water, and physical ease, which comprised the social agenda. Le Corbusier's "machine for living" has become realized in the pervasive presence of household appliances: refrigerators, washing machines, microwave ovens, dishwashers, trash compactors, hair dryers, and more.

The "typical" residential environment of the last decade of the 20th century is a rich, multicultural collage in which computers, electronic devices, and "sentimental" elements collide, though not always in a violent fashion. Family mementos from the past, books, photographs, paintings, and treasures may decorate walls and surfaces in our homes. Furniture that is now considered antique moves from home to home

as generations brachiate. Alienation and hostility limit personal interaction, yet, in our residential "enclaves" instant dialogue and affinity with strangers may occur via electronic nets.

Backyard gardens are protected by concertina wire. Lace and tulle drape industrial-grade shelves. A colonial-revival façade conceals computers, modems, facsimile machines, videocassette recorders, and digital cameras. Comfort in design is individually defined, usually by its ease of use, low maintenance, and reliability. Since the advent of film and photography, home is perceived as a controlled "set" for ourselves and families, in which traditions are reenacted—a reflection of our societal and cultural values, our moods and fantasies.

Architect Paola Iacucci, in a 1992 Berlin Spandau Wasserstadt essay, "Architecture and the City," states her belief that design should allow for invention: "The space of inhabitation can be a loft [or apartment] in which you make your own space, and the façade says nothing about you." A loft/home in New York City's Meat District, for instance, designed by

left Brooklyn, New York-based architect Jerzy Sulek is involved in rescuing parts of 19th-century buildings and incorporating them into sometimes jarring compositions on existing structures. The façade of a clapboard row house in the Greenpoint section of Brooklyn is a collage work of historic elements that offers an exciting visual statement.
photo Carla Breeze

below left Some contemporary designers appreciate the scarred remains of buildings, and are influenced by the look of ruin they present. Effects, such as those seen in a Los Angeles-area residential interior "destroyed" by fire, often are mimicked by on-the-edge design talents in spaces that challenge our traditional notions of beauty.
photo Carla Breeze

Ada Tolla and Giuseppe Lignano, is hacked out with wires and salvaged elements from the surrounding neighborhood, a visceral statement about electronic culture, with a nod to local aesthetics, but with little concern for the established notions of "beauty."

Unlike suburbs or smaller cities in the Northeast, home in New York City is generally limited to an interior space, an apartment, penthouse, or loft in a multistoried building. To have a traditional house requires land; even relatively freestanding brownstones built during the 19th century were more vertical than horizontal. Among early 20th-century modern architects, such as Le Corbusier and Frank Lloyd Wright, the future was envisioned with vast acreages of modern housing, to accommodate the masses equally, incorporating modern technology to improve the life of the "common" people. Existing structures forming traditional cityscapes were to be razed.

The ideas of New Modern are less dogmatic, and the social agenda has changed. Aspects of the original modern agenda,

however, allow for New Modern experimentation. Worries of the past have been answered, in the form of sanitation systems, the taken-for-granted delivery of potable water and electricity, otherwise known as infrastructure. The difference is in the presence of the past in contemporary design; modernists would have banished any traces of history in their schemes, New Modernists seemingly embrace it, while also addressing contemporary causes. Subordination of nature to the demand for

above The landscape of midtown Manhattan presents a melange of periods and styles. The information overload of the city's overall aesthetic, the inherent chaos of urban life, is embraced by many designers and architects whose work can be categorized as New Modern.

photo Carla Breeze

development and continual construction—Goethe's "Faustian model," in a sense—illustrates how large-scale building destroys the natural realm. Architects have responded to the existing crisis, adopting recycling, solar and other alternative energy, and new materials designed with conservation in mind. Technical, material, and spiritual forces transform building components into structures reflective of contemporary social life.

E-mail and bialys, modems and professional dog walkers, sleek skyscrapers towering over cobblestone streets—the unfinished edges in the city, where the culture shifts are always visible, never seamless. Lumbering toward the future, cast-iron facades may no longer conceal textile sweatshops, but residences. Hawley and Cook offer the "mulch theory," appropriate as an explanation of the "dynamic collapse" embodied in urban space. Accordingly, existing buildings, as well as the leftover spaces in between, often the result of technology or other societal shifts—vacant lots, railroad yards, etc.—can be infilled with residential projects.

The duality of the urban experience in many city cores is perceived at its most literal in the barrage of chaotic consumerism at the pedestrian level, sharply contrasted with the absolute uniformity of towering curtain walls above. The transient quality of this environment is combated at home, where visual and physical "comforts" are more consistent, informed by modes and styles that express family stability, intimacy, and privacy. A certain kind of tradition is available, that, due to uncontained population explosions, has been created for a mass market in which "familiar" homes and interior "stuff" are valued, though they have been given a stylish spin within a postmodern context.

In a nation of multicultures and international economics, tradition has many definitions. Competing tendencies, progressivism versus conservatism, romanticism versus classicism, have affected residential design over the past century, leaving unresolved the issue of the place of the machine in the human environment. Electronic communications have increased the dilemma. In the post-industrial world, no home

is replete without work space, it seems. A home is not just a place to live. Breyten Breytenbach, in an essay, "The Long March from Hearth to Heart," included in *Home: A Place in the World*, published in 1991 by the New School for Social Research, has written, "The individual creative act is certainly an attempt to make consciousness. This implies drawing upon memory. Memory, apocryphal or not, provides the feeding ground or the requisite space allowing for the outlining of imagination. Imagination is a biological necessity. The process is hazardous—but considerations such as free will, intentionality, escapism come into it, so that it can never be totally haphazard. Above all, the creative act aims to be narrative. The narrative is a feint trying to come to grips with chaos."

The anarchism implied by graffiti competes with personae defined by Gap clothing and the city grid. Perfection versus imperfection, frayed edges, rough finishes, and the pastiche of additions and repairs are explored in New Modern work. Tendencies in contemporary design work are divergent, but that divergence is tradi-

tional. In 1912, Umberto Boccioni's Futurist manifesto stated: "The straight line is the only means that can lead us to the primitive virginity of a new architectonic construction of sculptural masses and zones." Twenty-five years later, Jean Arp queried, "Why struggle for precision, purity, when they can never be attained?

above The look of historic vernacular buildings, such as this early 19th-century barn in Sandwich, New Hampshire, is often re-created, but with interiors designed for late-20th-century living. The shock of the new is sheathed by the familiar and nostalgic.
photo Carla Breeze

CONTEXT & ANTI-CONTEXT

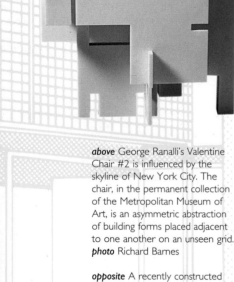

above George Ranalli's Valentine
Chair #2 is influenced by the
skyline of New York City. The
chair, in the permanent collection
of the Metropolitan Museum of
Art, is an asymmetric abstraction
of building forms placed adjacent
to one another on an unseen grid.
photo Richard Barnes

opposite A recently constructed
Colonial-style residence in Locust
Valley, New York, designed by
A. T. Gray Associates architect
Minor Bishop, borders on cliché in
terms of its contextual relationship with the surrounding traditional Eastern United States-style
suburban houses intended for
upper-middle-class consumption.
photo Courtesy of A. T. Gray
Associates

The New World awaiting colonists contained a wealth of natural resources, especially wood, a scarce commodity in Europe,
where deforestation had accrued over the
centuries. American colonial houses were
constructed of wood, using European techniques that had not changed since the 15th
century. The colonial style became an
architectural icon after the American
Revolution, with Classical references, ini-
tially Greek revival, used to symbolize the
new democracy. Americans were rapidly
re-creating themselves and their environments, their buildings reflective of the
change.

Regional/cultural influences and environmentally inspired solutions, as well as
developments in technology, were incorporated into American buildings over time,
but style was still very much focused on
classicism until the late 19th century. On
the fringe, vernacular styles, such as those
of the Shakers and other utopian communities who had discovered the beauty of
simple functionalism, were developed.
Generally, however, Americans were less
confident in their vernacular traditions
when status, wealth, and distinction needed to be conveyed. The trend of reviving
"traditional" New England colonial forms,
or what can be looked at as the progressive process of re-inventing American
style, was initiated with the Shingle style of
the late 19th century. The process continues into the 21st century.

Currently, slavish imitation is not the
goal of contextualists. Their references
may be allegorical or metaphorical.
Regional considerations may be deleted,
bringing the entire nature of the surrounding environment into question. While the
America of the past century has produced
its own culture, the underlying richness of
the culture at large is embodied in its vernacular traditions. A philosophy of anti-
context co-exists as a result of the con-
stant re-invention of what America is eco-
nomically and aesthetically.

Interiors of residential and commercial
buildings in cities and suburbs are continually modified. This modification includes
the amalgamation of several spaces, joining
two apartments to create one large area,
for instance. Traditions are as ambiguous
as the spaces themselves, and in the relationship between façade and interior. Solid
walls are rarely encountered. Transition
and stability are contradicted by raw steel
or sandblasted glass. Hints of the outdoors
come inside.

The Disneyesque fantasy of a traditional
home is treated as an absurd abstraction
by anti-contextualists. Standardized building materials, when applied to a tract house
or multiple-unit urban residence by con-
tractors and developers, rarely express
"uniqueness." Anti-context designers
embrace the mundane while going beyond
it, to provide an expression of individual-
ism. In the same way, the new breed of
contextualists mix up their metaphors, to
create a new look, in harmony with past,
but not enslaved by it.

right The Coxe Hayden House on Block Island, by Venturi, Scott Brown & Associates, incorporates traditional New England-style elements. Its identity as a contemporary structure isn't immediately apparent on its exterior, except in the subtle play of scale.
photo Tom Bernard

VENTURI, SCOTT BROWN & ASSOCIATES

Robert Venturi, Denise Scott Brown, and Steven Izenour have been involved with context and meaning since the 1960s. The Philadelphia-based team's realized and unbuilt projects have molded an entire generation of architects, who also read their seminal text, *Learning from Las Vegas*. In that book, the architects' analysis of the chaos of the Las Vegas commercial strip suggests that unity and order might exist, although we may not readily perceive the pattern. The architects are also interested in simple vernacular forms, which Venturi has lauded as the "ugly and ordinary." Venturi, Scott Brown & Associates creates familiar, yet complexly referential, residences and other buildings that are concerned with place, scale, history, and the semiotics of design.

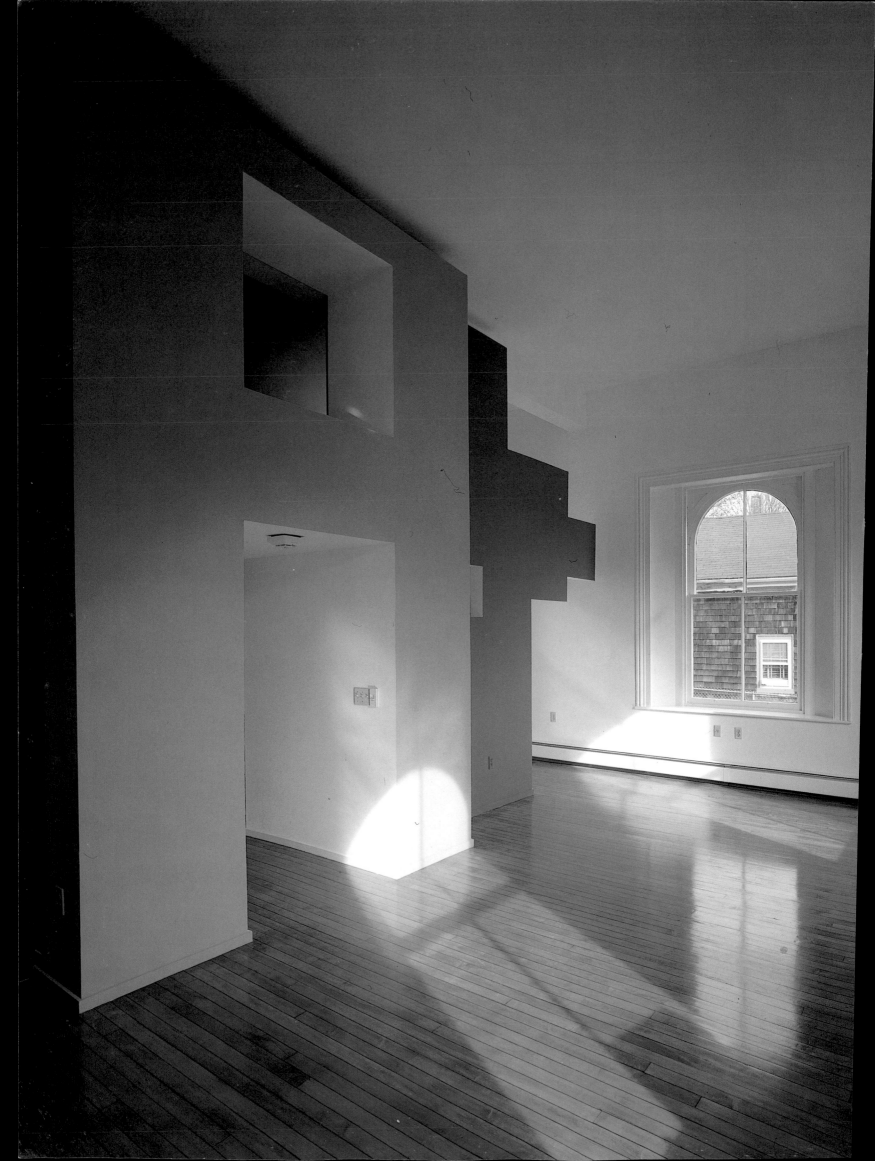

GEORGE RANALLI

Individuality has been a characteristic of American architects in the 20th century since Frank Lloyd Wright. Manhattan-based George Ranalli has developed a unique approach and an instantly identifiable style, conscious of the texture of the surrounding urban environment. His intriguing interlocking motif, informing many of his designs, is an abstraction of the geometric shadow patterns created by light interacting with the skyscrapers of New York City, but rotated vertically.

In a Princeton Architectural Press monograph on Ranalli's work, published in 1988, critic Anthony Vidler wrote this about the architect: "Refusing the literal quotation of defensive space, and any direct reference to pre-modern styles and motifs, Ranalli nevertheless describes a fundamentally post-modern condition. His shelters within shelters, freestanding or attached to their containers on one side, re-enact, so to speak, a primitive origin, reminiscent not of any anthropological source, but rather of those 18th-century myths of origin...."

Ranalli obtained a B.Arch degree from Pratt Institute in 1972, and an M.Arch from Harvard University's Graduate School of Design.

above In the renovation of the former Callender School into a residential loft building, Ranalli incorporated existing support elements into the formal composition of the interiors.
photo George Cserna

left The wall enclosing the kitchen in Ranalli's own loft space in Manhattan's Flatiron District is pierced and crenelated to a degree. The interior landscape explores the concepts of indoor/outdoor and public/private, within a space that was not built originally for housing.
photo George Cserna

background Interlocking forms in Ranalli's Manhattan office/studio create an almost kinetic structure within the confines of the space.
drawing Courtesy of George Ranalli, Architect

opposite Within the main living space of a Callender School unit, interior enclosures are treated by Ranalli like external walls.
photo George Cserna

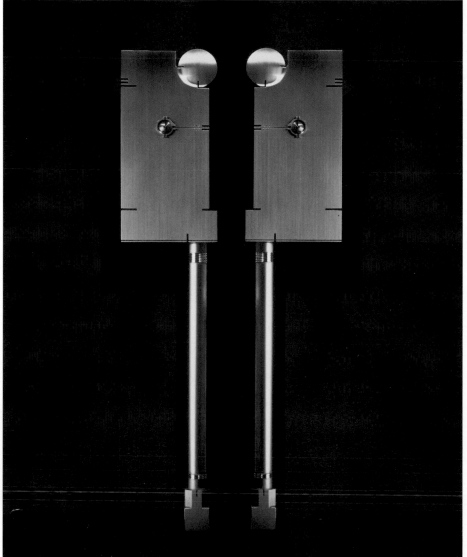

above "Windows" in the kitchen overlook the merged living and dining spaces in Ranalli's Manhattan loft.
photo George Cserna

left Ranalli was commissioned to create these door handles, which feature the interlocking shapes and forms he explores in his interiors, for the Union Company of Osaka, Japan.
photo William Whitehurst

opposite Ranalli incorporated forms garnered from his abstracted perception of the city and placed them on a hidden grid to create a striking interior effect in his studio.
photo George Cserna

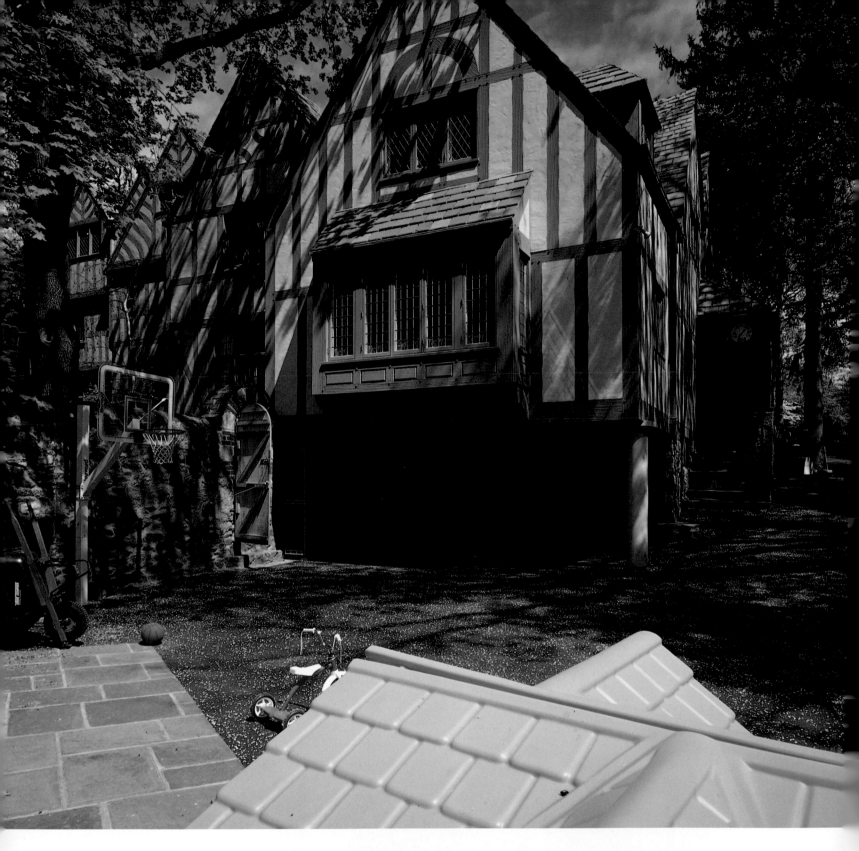

above In making an extensive addition to the Rappaport residence, a Bronxville, New York, house designed in the 1920s by Lewis Bowman, a master of the Tudor revival style, Bishop chose to fully embrace the existing style and structure, creating an almost undetectable new wing above the garage.
photo Carla Breeze

MINOR BISHOP

While attending architecture school at Yale during the height of the Miesian modern era Minor Bishop was considered to be an extreme eccentric—he was designing residences in the French provincial vein. Bishop was finally vindicated in 1994 during a New York Landmarks Conservancy function, when his nemesis, the venerable Yale architecture professor Vincent Scully, repudiated his earlier harsh criticism of Bishop's work by remarking that Bishop now represented the variety that was possible within the modern style, which no longer discards the past.

Bishop has designed numerous houses and additions to historic structures over the past 40 years. He is particularly fond of taking on renovations to houses designed by his idols, Lewis Bowman and Frank Forester, the prime protagonists of the Wall Street Pastoral style, who built stunning Tudor-revival and French-provincial houses in idyllic luxury suburbs like Greenwich, Connecticut, during the 1920s and '30s.

left The new children's playroom offers an authentically traditional appearance. Leaded-glass windows, beams, and moldings are in keeping with the interior details that exist in the portions of the original house.
photo Carla Breeze

below left Bishop also designed a separate pool house addition which includes a new-style traditional kitchen.
photo Carla Breeze

left While the kitchen in the Rappaport house addition is clearly a contemporary space, Bishop has incorporated new ceiling beams, lighting fixtures, tilework, and molded cabinet fronts that bring an old-fashioned quality to the room.
photo Carla Breeze

above The Indianapolis house Cornelius Alig designed for himself with colleague Deborah Berke presents a clean-lined version of the vernacular residential styles traditionally found in the Midwest. *photo* Gregory Murphey

CORNELIUS M. ALIG

Born in Indiana, Cornelius M. Alig is a real estate developer who graduated from Tulane University and received a Master of Science degree in Architecture and Urban Planning from Columbia University in 1982. After finishing his studies, he returned to Indianapolis to "tackle developing in-fill and historic preservation projects, which were then being overlooked.

In designing a house for himself and his wife, a textile conservator, in collaboration with architect Deborah Berke, Alig was determined to employ only local materials, a form of contextualism. "As a developer, I often see home builders buying plans from mail-order design firms that specify materials that are generally found all across the country," he says. "This trend, needless to say, encourages a standardization of design and specification that over time will parallel what we have already seen in commercial development—homogeneous cityscapes. It was important to me to avoid the conformity of this process and build a home that not only expressed a regional aesthetic, but also to use as many indigenous materials as I could for both interior and exterior."

The Alig residence straddles a narrow bluff 70 feet above the White River, defining an enclave within the wooded site. Through a modest vocabulary of forms and materials, the house establishes a balanced counterpoint with the landscape. The site is organized by a visual axis oriented directly toward the geographic center of Indianapolis. A breezeway bisects the house on this same axis, offering a framed view of the city's downtown area. The façades and interiors of the house reflect Alig's and Berke's elegant takes on Adolf Loosian Modernism, in which superfluous ornamentation is forbidden. The sensuous materials selected, however, are timeless.

above Rooms within the Alig residence, such as Dorothy Sites Alig's textile-conservation studio, are cleanly detailed, with few flourishes. Furnishings and finishes, such as the cork flooring in the studio, prevent the spaces from appearing too austere.
photo Gregory Murphey

left A certain elegance is conveyed through the simplicity of the interior architecture, combined with a choice selection of modern furnishings and works by regional artists, in the Alig living room.
photo Gregory Murphey

above & background Designed by Hardy Holzman Pfeiffer Associates, Highland House is composed of a cluster of connected smaller structures, rendered in a variety of vernacular forms.
photo Tom Kessler
drawing Courtesy of Hardy Holzman Pfeiffer Associates

opposite Sophisticated juxtapositions, involving symmetry, areas of color and materials, and balance, are explored throughout the interiors of Highland House, even heightening the impact of a rather spare appearing dining room.
photo Tom Kessler

HARDY HOLZMAN PFEIFFER ASSOCIATES

Committed to historic preservation and concomitantly to contemporary design, the Hardy Holzman Pfeiffer firm has produced an exciting range of work, mostly in the public and commercial realm. The firm's renovation of the Brooklyn Academy of Music's Majestic Theater and Rockefeller Center's Rainbow Room in the late 1980s initiated a reconsideration of historic preservation versus stabilization. In a recently published Rizzoli monograph on the firm's work, partner Hugh Hardy made this statement about the Rainbow Room renovation: "Our goal was not to make a confrontation between old and new but to see them integrated into a seamless whole...."

Hardy Holzman Pfeiffer's Highland House is a residence built in a Wisconsin suburb developed during the 1920s and filled with a variety of revival- and eclectic-style structures. To reflect its location, Highland House creates its own "village" atmosphere, facilitated by the formation of clusters of buildings in a crystalline-like growth pattern. To further the house's connection to the region, stone from a

Midwest cemetery was recycled as a building material. In environmentally aware New Modern style, only inert materials were used on the interior, eliminating the possibility of exposure to formaldehyde gases.

top The seemingly random window pattern in Highland House's living room is unexpected, yet adds a playful note to the interior, and is governed by the architects' desire for a particular composition on the exterior walls.
photo Tom Kessler

above & left Varied ceiling heights and treatments, touches of bright color, and a range of materials are enlisted to give the Highland House kitchen and adjoining living space an active demeanor, quite unlike the almost primary shapes that contain it from outside.
photos Tom Kessler

CHAPTER TWO

RECYCLING & ENVIRONMENT

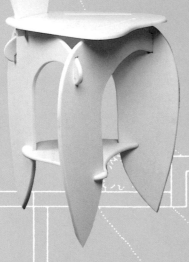

James Wines, who describes himself as an "artist working with architecture," was quoted in an April, 1992, *Metropolis* article, "The Seeds of a Green Architecture" as stating, "Architects never think about communication or the environment, even though these two thrusts are shaping the world. These issues should inspire the revolution of our time, just as industry and technology formed the original Modern movement."

Acknowledging the diminishing supply of nonrenewable natural resources—petroleum, varied species of wood and plants, as well as wildlife—has become an increasingly imperative matter. A large number of the architects and interior designers who can be categorized as New Moderns are extremely concerned about the diminishing supply of these elements.

Today, many architects and designers incorporate environmental consciousness into their work, exploring alternative energy sources, employing recycled materials, and rescuing existing structures through adaptive re-use projects. Yet, the recognition of recycling and environmental issues poses a particularly difficult challenge to members of the design community. While the American Institute of Architects publishes the *Environmental Resource Guide*, which covers such topics as site planning, new materials, energy conservation, and waste and building ecology, there are many alternative strategies yet to be addressed, and about which little information is available.

There are also paradoxes involved in so-called green design. For example, in some cases, post-consumer, recycled building and design materials may require more energy to produce than traditional, though irreplaceable, materials. Architects who consider environmental matters to be important are faced with a dilemma: if they are commissioned to design a brand-new structure, they have to decide if it is an environmentally sound move on their part, especially if the site is in an already densely overbuilt urban area. Should new structures be built at all? And, if constructed, how can recycling, recomposed materials, and energy conservation play a role?

American architects have been examining these and related issues since the 19th century. Orson Squire Fowler advocated the octagon shape as most conducive for a healthful living environment. Frank Lloyd Wright developed a low, linear building style influenced by and integrated with the prairie landscape. Bruce Goff worked with materials left over from World War II production efforts in several of his designs.

Today, there are hundreds of individuals, many of them architects and designers, a number of them artists, especially in the older cities along the Eastern Seaboard, who have, for themselves or their clients, become committed to the concept of architectural recycling. Older housing stock and manufacturing and other commercial spaces are being restored, updated, and converted as contemporary abodes. The residential loft, a housing type developed in relatively recent times, is the ultimate kind of urban renewal/recycling project: uninhabitable, usually abandoned, raw space is turned into spacious quarters for living and working.

above Utilizing post-consumer recycled plastic material, New York City-based designer/sculptor Henner Kuckuck created an easy-to-assemble chair.
photo Dan Nelken

opposite A New York City kitchen space, designed by Lot/Ek, has a post-industrial aesthetic, incorporating a variety of recycled and re-used found objects framed by elements made of untreated plywood and scrap lumber.
photo Ivan Terestchenko

opposite The Red Chair S1,
by Henner Kuckuck, is a light-
weight piece made of laminate,
rubber, aluminum, and leather.
A table and torchiere are similarly
composed. The wall sculpture
on the far right is actually the
knocked-down version of
Kuckuck's Spine Chair K1.
photo Rob Gray

left Working with Koroseal,
a new material for furniture,
Kuckuck has created the Spine
Chair K1, a collapsible, weather-
resistant seat that relies on a
metal frame for support.
photo Rob Gray

HENNER KUCKUCK

A graduate of the Hochscule für Bildende Künst, Berlin, now living in New York City, Henner Kuckuck is an artist, who, while working with sculpture, became interested in designing furniture and interiors. Formal, yet playful, Kuckuck's designs employ unexpected materials that are responsive to the environment, including aluminum and post-consumer recycled plastics. His furniture also addresses issues of weight, storage, and transport: many of his pieces are fabricated to be as light as possible, to reduce the amount of material consumed and to allow for shipping at the lowest rate possible, and several of them collapse to ship or store easily. Formica Corporation has supported Kuckuck's explorations into the use of recycled material.

"We live on this earth, it is our house, and we must take care of it," Kuckuck stated in conjunction with the recognition of his designs by the 38th Annual I.D. Design Review in 1992.

above & background The Moore House, a Connecticut residence designed by Alfredo De Vido Associates, almost disappears into the terrain. The house's sod roof, which requires intensified support because of its weight, provides excellent insulation, keeping the house cool in summer and warm in winter.
photo Norman McGrath
drawing Courtesy of Alfredo De Vido Associates

ALFREDO DE VIDO

For over 20 years, architect Alfredo De Vido has been dedicated to the idea of environmentally sound design. "I have designed a number of 'passive' solar houses, which sought to control the flow of thermal energy into, through, and out of the building by natural means, such as direct heat gain, sun space, siting, and orientation of the building, and the use of trombe and thermal massing," De Vido says.

For the Moore House residence, on a Connecticut site in the foothills of the Berkshires, De Vido, his assistant David Cook, and the clients determined that the house should not be placed atop a knoll, but should be nestled within it. In a discussion of the Moore project in the June 1993 issue of *Architecture*, De Vido explained that, "The house was sited not only to preserve the character of the land, but also in recognition of sound energy conservation principles. The house faces south and fits into the terrain in a manner that provides no exposure to the north. Using natural materials, sandblasted concrete, stone facings, and oak posts and beams, all rooms face south toward splendid views of the pond."

above In planning and constructing the Moore House, the architect and client consciously placed it to minimally disturb the natural setting.
photo Norman McGrath

left In the main living space, window walls bring as much of the landscape indoors as possible. Natural wood finishes are pervasive throughout the rooms of the house, such as the stock pine casements and cedar-surfaced ceilings.
photo Norman McGrath

right The piled-stone façade of the Moore House is in harmony with its site. The stone used was obtained from crumbling fences on the property.
photo Norman McGrath

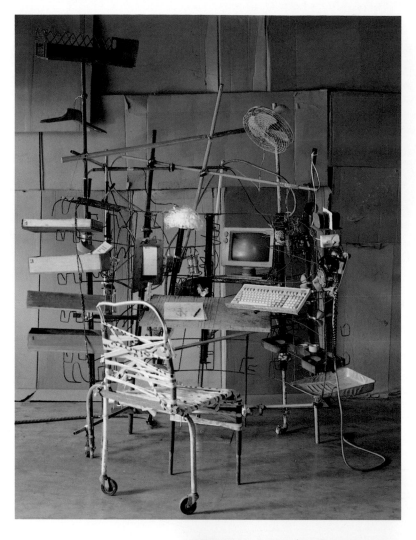

ADA TOLLA & GIUSEPPE LIGNANO (LOT/EK)

In response to a question regarding electrical engineering, architect Ada Tolla, partner with Giuseppe Lignano in Lot/Ek, confesses that she and Lignano do not allow their lack of expertise in this particular subject area to deter them from working with circuit boards, wiring, and other technological elements. By taking objects apart, she says, function and mechanics can be understood and, ultimately, subverted by the pair's design work. The furniture pieces designed by Lot/Ek are meant to be multifunctional—what they see as the wave for the next century.

Both Tolla and Lignano attended the University of Naples. They were awarded a grant to pursue post-graduate studies in architecture at Columbia University. Excited by the urban chaos of New York City, and the vast amount of cast-off resources available throughout the city, the pair decided to settle in Manhattan. Scavenged materials play an enormous role in the aesthetic the two have developed. In a feature published in the July 1994 issue of *Elle Decor*, they explained their philosophy of materials: "if you live in the countryside, nature provides you with trees. The city produces waste, so we use that for our designs."

Lot/Ek's first New York City project focused on the renovation of a former meat processing plant into a living/working loft for themselves. Zinc tubs used for washing meat became bath and kitchen sinks. The loft's floors are covered with metal signs found in the neighborhood. Their appreciation of found signage and, later, of other kinds of found graphics, led Tolla and Lignano toward the full development of the use of stenciled words as a part of their distinctive design vocabulary.

above A computer workstation designed by Lot/Ek for their own loft/studio is created from urban detritus.
photo Ivan Terestchenko

right Tolla and Lignano's own stereo lounger provides music, a reading light, and a comfortable place to sit—all within the framework of a cast-off mail cart.
photo Ivan Terestchenko

opposite Lot/Ek's renovation of the kitchen in Alessandra Alecci's brownstone in Manhattan's Chelsea district is representative of environmental recycling in its most literal sense. Innovative elements were made from wooden police barricades, metal signs, food crates, and other typically urban matter.
photo Ivan Terestchenko

left An abandoned meat-process-
ing plant in lower Manhattan
serves as the studio and residence
of the Lot/Ek team, who have
brought scavenging into the realm
of serious design. Much of the
''furniture'' in the loft was found
on-site, supplemented with colorful industrial materials and tools
picked up in the bins in front of
the hardware shops that line
Canal Street, a favorite haunt of
post-industrial pioneers such as
Tolla and Lignano.
photo Ivan Terestchenko

right Believing it better to recycle than contribute to deforestation by purchasing new furniture, McGee and Pecker used only pieces made by Pecker's father or found in the McGee family basement when they renovated their Brooklyn brownstone.
photo Carla Breeze

below McGee and Pecker exercised restraint during the renovation process, making sure that original details were kept intact, such as the wainscoting in a kitchen niche.
photo Carla Breeze

ELIZABETH A. McGEE & MARK S. PECKER

A noted feminist and contributor to *Our Bodies, Our Selves*, Elizabeth A. McGee wanted to make a home for her family in a century-old Park Slope, Brooklyn, brownstone, selected as much for its high ceilings as for its ample number of closets. Her husband, Mark S. Pecker, an associate professor of medicine at Cornell University and an internist on the staff of New York Hospital, felt it was important that they furnish their home with furniture made by his father and family members, along with a variety of pieces inherited from his wife's family. Neither McGee nor Pecker perceived the purchase of new furniture as environmentally correct, when these more meaningful pieces were readily available and recyclable for a new generation's use. The house's interior details, many of them original, have not been altered in McGee & Pecker's respectful reclamation of the property, where they reside with their two daughters.

above A 100-year-old wisteria shades the backyard's terrace and garden, which was cleaned up and landscaped to create an oasis amid the city's clamor at the same time that interiors were redone.
photo Carla Breeze

left Rooms in the McGee/Pecker residence, such as the library, have not been altered significantly in appreciation of the fine original architectural details.
photo Carla Breeze

IDI & JAN HENDERIKSE

Artists often create striking living/working environments within industrial or renovated residential buildings. Idi and Jan Henderikse, artists and educators, purchased a brownstone in the Fort Greene section of Brooklyn when they became disenchanted with the restrictions of apartment life in Greenwich Village. Their spacious recycled environment, in which original moldings and other interior details have been restored, is filled with work by both artists, as well as their collection of numerous pieces by other painters and sculptors.

above The interiors of the restored Fort Greene, Brooklyn, brownstone of Idi and Jan Henderikse have been embellished in the same manner an artist approaches a canvas. The architecture of the spaces is left pure, with elements imposed to create pleasing compositions, even in small corners and niches.
photo Carla Breeze

right Selected furniture, sculpture, and paintings make a striking statement throughout the Henderikse's brownstone. Their placement creates a pleasing vignette in this view of the living space. The standing ashtray is filled with ceramic cigars by Allen Daugherty; the chair is by Henner Kuckuck.
photo Carla Breeze

above The original plan of the brownstone has not been altered by the Henderikses. Smallish quarters, like this guest room, are used for multiple purposes: accommodating visitors and for storage of books, photographs, and finished artwork.
photo Carla Breeze

left On the brownstone's main living level, contemporary pieces are integrated into the fairly intact 19th-century interior envelope, with striking results.
photo Carla Breeze

below An apartment in a circa 1930s building on Manhattan's Upper West Side, designed by Georges, has become a setting for the client's collection of "recycled" family heirlooms and acquired pieces from the 1930s and 1940s.
photo Carla Breeze

opposite Tall glass doors have been added to separate living and kitchen/dining spaces, but are in keeping with the simple interior architecture of the apartment.
photo Carla Breeze

ANDRA GEORGES

Andra Georges's relocation to New York City from her beloved Los Angeles could only be ameliorated by "tearing out all the walls" of a 1930s-era Upper West Side apartment to capture the open feeling characteristic of living spaces in southern California. Georges does appreciate some aspects of the Manhattan-style apartment's past: In her redo of the pre-war residence, she has maintained many of the original architectural details, while incorporating several new elements, including new privacy-height cabinets and interior doors, for practical as well as aesthetic reasons.

A graduate of Yale University, Georges received her M.Arch degree from the University of California, Los Angeles. She has been working on several residential and commercial projects in New York City and on the West Coast.

above A soothing, yet colorful, palette has been chosen for the Upper West Side apartment, with pleasing details added to the original interior.
photo Carla Breeze

opposite A bookshelf storage unit, built to Georges's specifications, is placed strategically to divide the living room and a newly created entry area. While not necessarily traditional in style, the divider revives the concept of a traditional home, in which one encounters a succession of rooms from the front hall through to other parts of a residence, from reception to public to more private spaces.
photo Carla Breeze

HEAVY METAL & INDUSTRY

5

Beaten, cut, cast, and formed, metal has served and decorated the human body and environment since the Bronze Age. Today, among the "cool" trendsetters in New York City's East Village, metal is as ubiquitous as black leather. In this neighborhood, metal grommets, rings, and studs pierce every conceivable realm of flesh. Denizens strolling its streets provoke a sinister response. Mall rats, too, all over the United States, have adopted this look, an especially odd note in otherwise bland suburbia.

In the structures of contemporary commercial and domestic buildings, metal is an essential, and very modern, component. Steel curtain walls, metal girders, and cast-iron façades have given the urban environment a hard edge. Base metals and alloys appear in myriad forms, types, and stylings. It is logical that metal treatments have also made their ways indoors, appreciated for their industrial-strength quality and particular toughness, both physically and visually.

The entrance to the Pat Hearn Gallery in Manhattan's Alphabet City, done up in an assemblage of metal and metallic forms, struck a chord a few years back. It was considered beautiful, durable, easy to maintain, and secure, in reality as well as in appearance. Metal isn't just a "downtown" phenomenon, however, and has slowly migrated into more elite quarters. French designer Philippe Starck used stainless steel elements for the interiors of the Royalton Hotel in midtown Manhattan, which caters to a decidedly uptown audience. Its pièce de résistance is, perhaps, its lobby men's room, wherein a sleek wall of stainless steel, flushed with a sheet of water serves as a startling urinal.

In a 1992 U.S. Department of the Interior publication, *Metals in America's Historic Buildings*, authors Margot Gayle and David W. Look point out that stainless steel has been used since the Second World War for counters, hospital surfaces, and other industrial spaces in the United States. The "romance" many architects and interior designers have developed with industry and technology has inspired them to go beyond the industrial use of stainless steel and other metals, bringing these materials into the residential context. Since the 1970s, when the High-Tech style first emerged, a New Modern generation, less concerned with sleekly "finished" industrial spaces, has come forward to claim metals and other formerly industry-exclusive substances—concrete, rubber, wire, and Fiberglas, among others—as their materials of choice. The process of working and shaping materials is not concealed. Welding burns and etched, scratched, or buffed surfaces and other fabrication techniques purposely remain evident. The mannerisms of mere style are vehemently opposed; New Modern designers take a more militant approach toward the idea of materials honesty.

The early 20th-century concern for veracity exposed the process of building, and created the appreciation for materials versus "superfluous" ornament. Often, however, the almost dogmatic touting of the simplicity implied by the use of industrial materials and their modular modernity was only symbolic.

Symbolic adherence to modernity has become less pervasive as modernism has become totally integrated into mainstream architectural and design practices, as opposed to remaining an avant-garde concept. Materials used by New Modern architects and designers are chosen for practical concerns: stability, ability to withstand environmental stress, maintenance type and cost requirements, among others. The so-called machine-shop aesthetic is often dictated by economic considerations as well, always a challenge in creating impactful, yet affordable, places to live and to work, with industrial components chosen over comparable domestic-use products because of their ability to withstand greater use and abuse over time.

below Though not yet built, a residence in New Jersey designed by Frank Lupo and Dan Rowen is intended to incorporate industrial-grade materials for a hard-edged, tactile appeal, in a plan that flows more sensuously than one would expect.
photo & drawing Courtesy of Frank Lupo & Dan Rowen Architects

opposite The Stockton/Lupo Brooklyn residence fills a space formerly used as a bay for loading and unloading trucks. Selected colors and furnishings soften the space, though its origins are celebrated through several elements, either existing or designed specifically for it.
photo Andrew Garn

background Lupo & Rowen's design for a New Jersey residence, shown in plan and sections, was to have explored the use of numerous "modern" industrial materials.
drawings Courtesy of Frank Lupo and Daniel Rowen Architects

below A color sketch for the unbuilt New Jersey house shows the architects' conception for the effective combination of a variety of surfaces.
sketch Courtesy of Frank Lupo and Daniel Rowen Architects

opposite As Lupo and Stockton were unable to alter or conceal the concrete truck dock in the warehouse space they converted into the residence, the resulting bi-level main living area is not only ample, but remains true to its origins.
photo Andrew Garn

MARY EVELYN STOCKTON, FRANK LUPO, & DANIEL ROWEN

Since receiving her M.Arch degree from Yale, Mary Evelyn Stockton has worked on several important architectural projects, including Cesar Pelli's World Financial Center complex in lower Manhattan. She discovered the former beer warehouse in Brooklyn, which she and Frank Lupo, who also holds an M.Arch from Yale, converted into a living space for themselves. The renovation of the warehouse's loading-dock space, built to accommodate high-clearance delivery trucks, into a feasible place to reside was a process involving many challenges and unique solutions. Looking at the warehouse's industrial-grade columns and fenestration as the "building blocks of a lifetime," as they informed a writer from Metropolitan Home in 1990, Stockton and Lupo worked to create a new kind of domestic environment, while maintaining the space's original industrial-based integrity. A dispatcher's office became the bedroom. The truck parking area and loading dock became a two-level main living, dining, and gallery space. The overall envelope was left intact, with a series of interior structures added.

Lupo shares an office with architect Daniel Rowen in New York City. Both work primarily in the residential design realm. They met while both were employed in the office of Gwathmey Siegel & Associates. Their collaborations include several projects in which industrial materials, unusual colorations, and a clean Modern-based aesthetic are explored, some built, some existing only as ideas on paper—the dilemma faced by young architectural practices. Lupo explains, "I strive to create timeless and well-considered architecture....My point of departure is Modernism and I am committed to the use of materials and methods that endure."

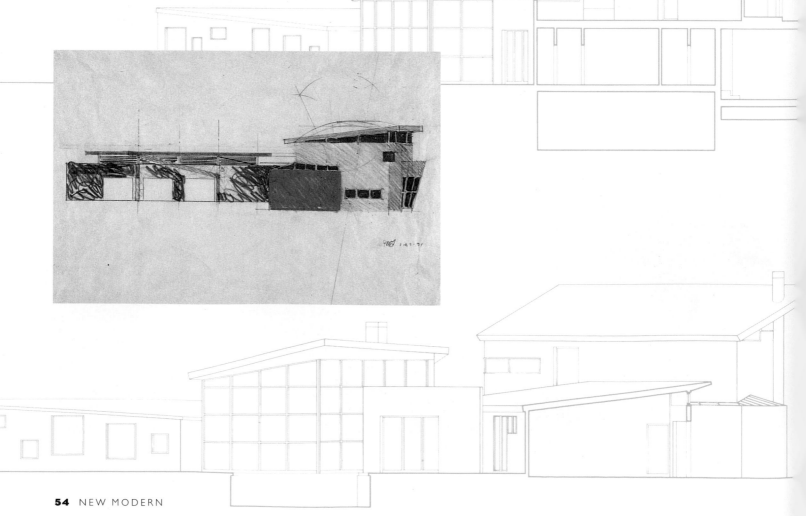

below, right, & opposite An abandoned remnant from the Baby Boom era, the Claflin Elementary School in Newton, Massachusetts, was purchased by a group of artists as a place to live and work. Patricia and Wellington Reiter reside and work in a space that was formerly half of the school's gymnasium. They wanted to exploit the height of the skylit space and created a partial second level, its "rooms" connected by industrial-strength catwalks and reached via warehouse-style steps and ladders.
photos Brian Vanden Brink
drawing Courtesy of Reiter & Reiter

REITER & REITER

Architect Patricia Reiter has been involved with historic preservation and housing issues since graduation from the University of Tennessee. She later earned her M.Arch degree from the Harvard University Graduate School of Design. While living in Knoxville, Reiter nominated and surveyed Tennessee's first designated historic district, the Mechanicsville neighborhood. With Wellington Reiter, a graduate of Harvard's Graduate School of Design and an artist-architect, she founded their eponymous architecture and design firm, which has taken on commercial and residential commissions. Wellington Reiter has been working with architectural-scale sculpture, and his installations have appeared at ArtPark in Lewiston, New York, Parsons School of Design in New York City, and the Akin Gallery in Boston. A recent residential project undertaken by the pair encompassed the conversion of spaces in a former elementary school into housing for artists, including their own living/working space in the school's former gymnasium. In describing the Howcroft/Maren loft unit they designed within the building, the Reiters state that the finished residence represents, "the resolution of the conflicting goals of creating a traditional living space within a raw open space, while preserving its industrial characteristics."

above A shipshape industrial aesthetic guided Reiter & Reiter in their design of the Howcroft/Maren loft, in another part of the now residential Claflin School.
photo Clements Howcroft

left Extensive areas covered in natural-finish wood in the Reiters' loft-style space refer to its school gymnasium ancestry. A wall of raw sheet metal encloses a "building within the building," its second floor reached by a ladder-style walkway.
photo Brian Vanden Brink

JOHN MYER

A pastoral view of stone-flecked fields filled with wild aster and Queen Anne's lace is interrupted by an aluminum-clad "bent" structure. The rocky terrain and temperamental climate at the base of the White Mountains cradle John Myer's Pasture House in Sandwich, New Hampshire. "Different from the traditional New England house form, which has an identity independent of its landscape, the bent-frames, or bents, are one aspect of a form of which the landscape is the other," explains Myer. "Together, they form an identity of place."

The architect continues: "In this south-facing pasture, the house hunkers down in the land for protection during the winter. It forms a cave opening to the south, the vast view, and the low winter sun. The pasture—a composition of boulders, juniper, shrubs, grass, fir, and spruce—is terraced near the building to create level ground for gardens, plazas, parking, and the house itself. Some boulders were pushed aside to permit use of the site, then joined by even larger boulders to reinforce and intensify the theme. In some ways, the rounded boulders left by the Ice Age are like us, temporary visitors on the scene. In time, gravity will again move them, as well as us, downhill.

"The interior is organized for year-round use. In winter, the well-insulated interior takes in passive solar heat via the vertical glazing in southern-exposure, double-pane windows, which is then stored in thermal reservoirs—the fireplace mass of concrete, the floor slab, and the earth below the foundation. Protected from ground frost by a 4-foot skirt of 2-inch foam board, the foundation is a shallow 2½ feet. This system keeps the house between 45 and 55 degrees most of the winter, requiring only two cords of wood to bring it above 70 degrees. A back-up system of electrical heat via ceiling radiation coils turns on if the temperature inside the house drops to 40 degrees or less, protecting plumbing from freezing.

"In the summer cycle, the living room skylight is covered and the thermal masonry and earth mass serve to cool the house. The screened east porch provides the welcome comfort of being outdoors."

above & left Architect John Myer has embraced industrial-grade materials to make for a comfortable as well as energy-conscious environment at Pasture House. Eroded walls soften the impact of concrete. Dowels plugged into the wall surface serve as towel hooks for a nearby outdoor shower.
photo Carla Breeze
drawing Courtesy of John Myer

below Concrete, metal, and wood clad the exterior of Pasture House.
photo Carla Breeze

opposite The south-facing façade features a wall fenestration to take advantage of warmth and light year-round. Shoji-style screens above the dining area off the kitchen can be opened to allow in extra natural light in winter or closed in summer to shield the interior from excessive heat.
photo Carla Breeze

top Pasture House is nestled into a hill, for added insulation against the elements. Huge boulders were added to the landscape to soften the hard-edged lines of the roof. *photo* Carla Breeze

above & left The screened pergola is designed for summertime living. The raw, almost brutal, quality of the interior is softened by wooden elements and furnishings. Concrete walls have been jackhammered in several places to reveal stones embedded beneath the surface. *photos* Carla Breeze

above Myer gave the fireplace
in the main living space a massing
that is meant to retain as much
heat as possible, both from the
fire itself and sunlight that hits it.
photo Carla Breeze

above Hard and soft, brutal and delicate elements are juxtaposed in the living room.
photo Carla Breeze

left Kitchen shelving, constructed of untreated wood in a Japanese-influenced post-and-lintel style, is lit from above by roof windows.
photo Carla Breeze

below & opposite Lauretta
Vinciarelli explores the effect of
light and space in her paintings
and her downtown Manhattan
loft, which was left fairly raw after
conversion from light manufacturing use. Shown below is a work
titled "For Peter."
photos Carla Breeze

LAURETTA VINCIARELLI

Similar to architects who produce primarily theoretical work, artist/architect
Lauretta Vinciarelli paints places that exist
in her mind and are "built" on paper. All
these "spaces" are suffused with serenity
and a sense of order. Vinciarelli holds a
doctorate in architecture and urban planning from the University of Rome, and has
worked as an architect in Italy and the
United States.

An accomplished painter, her canvases
are in the permanent collection of the
Museum of Modern Art, New York. She
has worked on many collaborative projects, including a conceptual space created
with artist Donald Judd, a "Library for the
Work of All Living Poets," commissioned
by the Dia Art Foundation.

Writing about Vinciarelli's masterful
series of watercolors published in *The
Architecture of Light*, critic Lebbeus Woods,
in *A+U*, perceived her work to be, "testimony to the existence of spirit and to the
humanistic possibilities of feeling that can
still be called religious...these images of
architecture recall the fervor of
Modernism when it was at its fervent best,
yet add something more: a skepticism
about modern culture that brings these
images and architecture to a pitch of intensity that could exist only now."

Woods continues, "The space she draws
is emptied of the paraphernalia of day-to-
day living, of overused symbols, and the
usual signs of a search for meaning.
Vinciarelli has no use for the shallowness of
gratuitous passions and throw-away
trends. She also understands that in a plu-
ralistic culture, traditional symbols can no

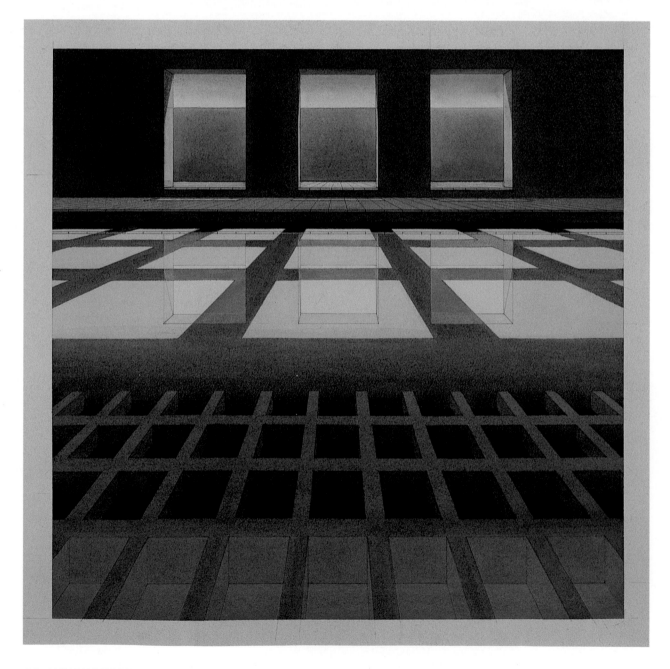

above & right The only walls in the Vinciarelli loft enclose sleeping chambers and storage areas, with a curved wall to allow for unusual plays of light and shadow. Original columns are left untreated, providing a certain rhythm in the space. The circular stair was a practical addition.
photos Carla Breeze

longer be used with the force of conviction, but can only be cheaply exploited, as in the typical post-Modern pastiche of diverse cultural elements."

In the design of her own Manhattan loft and studio space, Vinciarelli has adopted many of the ideas presented in her two-dimensional work into the third dimension. It is left fairly raw, with the play of light and shadow, perspective, and forms and voids enhanced to create its distinct atmospherics.

above & opposite Vinciarelli's loft residence and studio features soaring high ceilings topped with sprinkler pipes and warehouse-style lighting fixtures, and original exposed under-window radiators. Floors have been refinished, but are valued for their uneven texture.
photos Carla Breeze

above A former TriBeCa manufacturing space has been converted into Mills's residence. A dividing wall between the living area and kitchen is layered for an interesting effect, with a small interior window adding to the architectural composition. Mills designed the post-Modern-style sofa.
photo Carla Breeze

drawing Mills conceived the Melnick Residence in Brighton, Michigan, as a passive-solar structure. "The house is set into a hill so that it is virtually invisible upon approach," says the architect. "The central space of the house is a full-height gallery that runs the full length from the entry porch to a framed view of the lake at its lowest point.
drawings Courtesy of Edward I. Mills

EDWARD I. MILLS

Sensual interplays between materials and textural juxtapositions inform the work of New York City-based architect Edward I. Mills. Mills received his M.Arch degree from Harvard. He worked for the well-known architecture firms I.M. Pei & Partners and Richard Meier, Architect, before opening a design office in the post-modern-era 1980s with colleague Bartholomew Voorsanger. Mills now heads his own solo Manhattan practice.

Mills's residential work is concerned with issues of energy-efficiency and materials innovation. His designs have promoted the innovative application of generic vernacular and industrial materials. In his own New York City loft, the architect has creatively embellished the industrial traces of the space with impressive results.

above A freestanding curved screen, made of translucent industrial plastic stretched across a wooden framework, separates living and dining areas in Mills's TriBeCa loft.
photo Carla Breeze

left Mills has imposed architectural elements into the space, altering its character somewhat, while retaining many of its original factory details.
photo Carla Breeze

above A variety of materials is incorporated throughout the living/dining space of the Gilbane Residence.
photo Paul Warchol

left In the Gilbane bedroom, walls of pink granite, slick woods, and the fieldstone play off one another for an exciting spatial effect.
photo Paul Warchol

background Concord House, designed with Douglas Dolezal and Peter Lofgren, explores juxtapositions of layers of materials and textures.
drawing Courtesy of Machado & Silvetti

opposite In the hands of Machado & Silvetti, what might seem to be clashing materials, some thought of as strictly for use as exterior cladding, are brought together to create a kind of visual harmony inside.
photo Paul Warchol

MACHADO & SILVETTI

Rodolfo Machado and Jorge Silvetti masterfully integrate materials of seemingly disparate natures, orchestrating montages of conventional and unconventional elements. Raw and finished, these combined materials bring a distinct and affecting texture to the pair's projects. Machado & Silvetti's work has been labeled "Cubist," due to the interlocking layers and striking juxtapositions created on the inside and outside of their structures.

In the Gilbane residence, the architects used an L-shaped plan to create zones of privacy, separating private and public spaces effectively, though they are open to one another. Machado & Silvetti are very interested in plays with perspective; the long hallways and glimpses from room to room in the Gilbane project investigate this concept. References to New England ver-

nacular are seen in clapboard and granite walls, as well as the inherent concept of thrift adopted, and the use of odds and ends. Recent projects, such as Concord House in Massachusetts, are focused on orchestrating a montage of conventional as well as unconventional elements.

POP

opposite The shape of the structure that houses the master bedroom of architect Lee Skolnick's Sag Harbor, New York, house is repeated in the shape of the fireplace, in what might be construed as a celebration of particularly familiar form.
photo Carla Breeze

Defying former definitions of art, architecture, and aesthetics, Pop describes the cult of the known, the realm of desire and consumerism. Pop has been defined since the 1960s, as a reverence for the attitudes inherent in the popular culture of the United States—advertising imagery and techniques, marketing vocabulary, and the media of comic books, movies, and pulp novels.

Despite the whimsy of Andy Warhol, Pop is not without its intellectual and poetic qualities. Painter Jasper Johns, also known as a purveyor of Pop, stated that he saw himself in a dream painting an American flag before he actually did, lending some mysticism to his famous series of American flag paintings. Johns was involved in the process of painting, using difficult techniques such as encaustic to create works presenting fairly peripheral, Pop subjects. He did, however, accomplish on the surface what Warhol's more superficial work was involved with, the elevation of simple, relatively mundane items depicted

to the level of universal icon.

Pop gives generic objects new life, a perspective unintended by the original manufacturer or designer. Consider sculptor Claes Oldenburg's giant turning wing nut, clothespin, and lipsticks, or Warhol's Campbell's Soup cans and Brillo boxes. Playing with the scale of an ordinary object, enlarging it or removing it from "normal" context, manipulates the viewer's perception of it.

Paul Carroll's 1968 interview with Oldenburg, titled "The Poetry of Scale," published in a book about the artist's work, *Proposed Monuments and Buildings: 1965-69*, released by the Ryerson Press in 1969, reveals the artist's belief in the fetishistic power of objects. The material culture, which Pop confronts, continues to exert an influence on architecture, attesting to the power of simple icons and messages, if not the fetishistic power of objects.

Pop elements, like any other influences from the visual and literary arts, take time to make their way into the realm of the built environment because of the expense of building. That such influences are manifested in architecture long after their initial appearance, is a reflection of the role clients play—patrons and financiers of the design and construction of a particular project. For younger architects and designers especially, the role of the client is critical, since the client must be willing to take chances on experimental work. That they have is testimony to the strength and perseverance of New Modern architects and designers.

The Pop design aesthetic is bright and cheery in a tongue-in-cheek fashion. It is concerned with scale, incorporates any number of recollections and retakes of the past, and is innovative in terms of materials used and the transformation of manufactured elements beyond their expected place.

above Constantin Boym laminated actual books to construct his Coffee-Table Book Tables, part of the designer's "Searstyle" collection—a commentary on popular taste.
photo Courtesy of Boym Studio

right The Searstyle sofa in Boym's Manhattan apartment is covered in a woodgrain-patterned fabric, with back cushions of "found" corduroy backrest pillows. The designer has explored the mundane, the everyday, in this particular collection of furniture.
photo Carla Breeze

opposite The Komar & Melamid studio/loft in lower Manhattan, designed by Boym, translates Pop Art concepts into three dimensions, with a decidedly perverse sense of Russian humor. The main room features bright red folding chairs surrounding a red star-shaped table, and a series of mass-produced busts of Stalin and Jesus Christ.

CONSTANTIN BOYM

A graduate of the Moscow Architectural Institute and Domus Academy in Milan, Russian-born Constantin Boym has created a variety of projects and objects influenced by and exploring popular culture, both American and Russian. Before Boym opened his own practice in New York City—he is now an American citizen—he worked in the office of architect Graham Gund.

When asked what book he would place in the hands of every Russian, Franklin Delano Roosevelt responded, "The Sears & Roebuck Catalogue." Inspired by this, Boym decided recently to explore what he terms "Searstyle," taking Roosevelt literally at his work. He wanted to create products that would mollify the harshest "kulture kritik"; the avant garde, as well as many persons of so-called taste, have bemoaned the kitsch of Sears furniture. Boym was driven to challenge that presumption by producing furniture and interiors that demonstrated an "economy of means," certainly an admirable Modernist goal, while presenting an array of pieces that are clever and express a somewhat knowing design attitude.

With Searstyle, as well as in his other work, Boym can be seen as continuing the trend first initiated by Venturi, Scott Brown & Associates, with their appreciation for "bad" architecture. Boym validates popular culture with creative torque.

above Leon has designed a line of "narrative" appliances, on display in her undesigned typical Manhattan kitchen: The gingham-covered "Dorothy" toaster; "Tin Man" espresso machine; and "Wicked Witch" blender.
photo Carla Breeze

LAURENE LEON

Laurene Leon designs kitchen appliances that go beyond the typical functional ideal strived for by industrial designers throughout the 20th century. She is interested in the narrative qualities of design, incorporating references to television, movies, and novels into the forms of coffeepots and other household "conveniences."

Leon's projects confront the inherent power of object fetishization. Our housewares, objets d'art, and furniture are equated with ourselves. It is, consequently, consistent that our own narratives should shape the domestic products and appliances that we use.

In her "Wizard of Oz" series, the technology represented by a blender is humanized, for instance, by coloring its blades in the same tone as the Wicked Witch's green fingernails, making the object something to appreciate beyond its functional beauty and practicality. Subsequently, it has been given a life of its own, something to tie it to the individual user or admirer. Leon, who obtained a master's degree in industrial design from Pratt Institute, is attracted to the idea of creating objects that concentrate on the cultural aspects of design only. Her choice of culture happens to be cinematic Pop.

left & below The pink "Glinda" ice cream freezer and "Scarecrow" crock pot, shown at left, and the dishwasher design below are also part of Leon's "Oz" appliance line, which introduces a touch of whimsy into the realm of usually dead serious, practicality-rich industrial design.
photos Carla Breeze, Keith Piacensy

CHARLES R. MYER

Charles Myer's work is highly conscious of secondary use, durable materials and historical memory. Cornwall House, in Connecticut, which he renovated and expanded, was originally constructed in 1929 from plans and building materials purchased out of the Sears & Roebuck mail-order catalogue.

Mail-order houses could be selected during the first four decades of the 20th century from a special Sears catalogue, the Book of Modern Homes and Building Plans. Prices for these house kits, which included plans, specifications, lumber, and nails, were accordingly modest, from

$2,000 to $3,500. Each component was numbered to facilitate construction. Mail-order houses came in a variety of traditional styles.

Cornwall House rests on the side of a hill, bathed in the warmth of a southern exposure. It occupies a 5-acre plot that was a working dairy until purchased by a landscape painter and her writer husband, who now use it as a second home and studio. In 1989, the owners decided to completely renovate the house, adding 500 square feet to the interior. Their aim in undertaking the renovation was specific: The addition should preserve the scale of the original structure and enhance its

above & opposite The kitchen of Myer's Cornwall House is equipped with new cabinetry, painted in a green tone popular during the 1930s. Though geared toward contemporary needs, the room has an overall nostalgic flavor.
photos Carla Breeze

background Elevation of Cornwall House interior.
drawing Courtesy of Charles R. Myer

right & opposite Many walls within Cornwall House have been removed to open up the interiors significantly. The kitchen and dining room, furnished with 1950s-era "antique" pieces, can be seen from what was once an enclosed interior stairway.
photos Carla Breeze

relationship with the surrounding landscape.

Myer, who took on the job, came up with an elegantly designed and engineered solution for the house expansion. He added a second floor, too heavy to be supported by the existing walls, that floats above the walls on a series of new columns. He unified the renovated house with a two-story-high, nine-foot wide "spine" that juts through the original roof at its ridge. The rooms of the house, on both levels, open to this circulation spine. A view through the full length of the house, culminating in a picture window framing a clematis-covered shed in the rear garden, can be seen from the front-door entrance hall. Along the full length of the north and south sides of the double-height space are operable clerestory windows, which provide cross-ventilation and funnel sunlight into the center of the house. Below, the living room, dining room, and kitchen all feed up into this space, drawing on its light.

The foremost Pop characteristic of the house is the fact that it was originally a mass-market "product." Myer has lightened its interior spaces considerably, with touches of bright color that, while selected for their period authenticity, also bring a Pop sensibility to the experience of the house.

Myer has an M.Arch degree from the University of California, Los Angeles. He also holds a master's degree in real estate development from the Massachusetts Institute of Technology.

top A screened porch is in keeping with the nostalgic tone Myer has set throughout the project.
photo Carla Breeze

above Spaces in Cornwall House are simple and filled with references to aesthetics associated with the past. The breakfast room overlooks a cottage-style garden.
photo Carla Breeze

opposite Bright, clear primary and secondary colors are used to bring out the details within the clean-lined interiors.
photo Carla Breeze

background Cornwall House, in elevation, offers a simple form that is almost the iconic American house.
drawing Courtesy of Charles R. Myer

below Sag Harbor House is composed of various forms attached
to a whole. A fireplace chimney-
shaped room, clad in coppered
lead panels, brings to mind the
public-scaled works of Pop artist
Claes Oldenburg.
photo Carla Breeze

opposite Layering materials masterfully, Skolnick juxtaposes fossil-
laden marble and various woods
in the living room.
photo Carla Breeze

LEE H. SKOLNICK

Sag Harbor House, on the South Fork of eastern Long Island, is a pyrotechnical display of form and material. Located on a promontory, the house progresses laterally to take advantage of cross-ventilation and a spectacular view of the sea. Inspired by Japanese architecture, Lee Skolnick developed a concept of connecting a small, intimate series of spaces in a minimal landscape. Details, such as brass *V* drain pipes and small rock gardens, are integrated with the exterior to separate forms. Materials are brick, mahogany, fieldstone, lead-coated copper, which has an almost opalescent blue purple sheen, and copper sheeting, normally used on roofs.

Once attached to the utopian vision of Paolo Soleri, Skolnick worked with the artist/architect in Arizona for a summer years ago. He returned to New York City, graduating from The Cooper Union's School of Architecture. Based in Sag Harbor, Skolnick has become the architect of choice among many of the artists who settle in the Hamptons.

Memory and sentiment are qualities inherent to pop culture, as well as to the work influenced by it. Skolnick's poetic forms allude to these qualities. At Sag Harbor House, Skolnick's studio is accessible only by an external stairway or ladder, like a lifeguard tower or lighthouse. Use of mahogany in the dining room recalls the interior of a sailing ship cabin. A Cape Cod

saltbox form is placed at the second-floor level. Its scale, as well as the historical allusion it represents, is Pop, as is a large chimney form amusingly placed in the "foreground" of the artistically composed structure.

Eero Saarinen said, "A great building makes a great ruin." Skolnick seems to keep that in mind, choosing materials that he expects to weather well and that require minimal maintenance. Many New Moderns, like Skolnick, acknowledge and accept, even encourage, time's processes and marks on buildings.

right Brick, stone, metal, glass, and wood clapboard work together on the interior and exterior of Sag Harbor House. This breeze-way connects the guest wing and studio to the main house.
photo Carla Breeze

below right Traditional materials are used in striking new ways within Sag Harbor House. The living room is furnished in eclectic fashion, mirroring the designer's coherent blending of old and new.
photo Carla Breeze

far right The breakfast room off the kitchen is clean without being severe. Warmth is provided via the selection of old-fashioned furnishings.
photo Carla Breeze

above A child's bedroom offers
bright floral wallpapers under an
open-trusswork ceiling.
photo Carla Breeze

above Skolnick's Sag Harbor
House studio space, reached
via an exterior stair or ladder, is
placed almost precariously over
the guest wing. The structure
is reminiscent of traditional
beachside shacks, though more
consciously sophisticated.
photo Carla Breeze

MAVERICKS

below The Chopstick, a table lamp
designed by Henner Kuckuck,
employs simple materials in an
economic fashion.
photo Dan Nelken

opposite Architect Donald
Billinkoff created a new rhythm
within the interior of a Greenwich
Village town house he renovated.
A semi-circular stairway and railing
to one side of the main level is
open to ground-level living spaces.
The thoroughly contemporary
envelope is set off with traditional
furniture forms and floral patterns.
photo Carla Breeze

Only a nation of mavericks could have created one of the most heterogeneous and highly industrialized cultures out of the vast wilderness of the North American continent. Historically, the essence of American culture has been rough-hewn individuality. Upstarts abounded as well. Getting "there" first preoccupied 19th-century Americans, whether they were settling the West or building the transcontinental railroad.

Being first and advertising that fact has also become a predominant characteristic among Americans throughout the 20th century. In the 1990s, the "frontiers" are found in urban centers, where educational facilities, infrastructure, and viable public spaces have been eroded—places where small children carry weapons and shoot-outs occur frequently.

Design mavericks are facing these issues, along the crumbling waterfronts and in virtually empty industrial skeletons in New York City, Boston, and other metropolitan areas. To these new iconoclasts, the urban ruin is a viable, and preferable, alternative to franchise architecture and contract housing.

Artists, architects, and industrial designers, these mavericks are confronting urban development and infrastructure reconstruction in a way that embodies the Mephistolian contradiction of destruction and renewal. Mavericks often homestead areas of intense urban decay. Aware of historical precedents, they often employ recycled materials (post-consumer, found, or in situ) and ephemeral means to accommodate the environment and meet their needs. Mavericks are not simple to categorize, however. For some, fastidious attention to detail often is eschewed, with convenience and expediency overriding traditional craftsmanship; for others, austere and often rather slick means are essential to their design approaches.

Insipid suburbs and video arcades have produced these mavericks. The handmade object is part of their prevailing ethic, especially when surrounded by manufactured goods and environments built in the service of commercialism. Ethnic references are deemed more relevant than characterless, anonymous houses and housewares. Ecological concepts are important, too, but not in a superficial way. "Eco-style" boutiques mean less to the maverick than concrete applications of legislation and actions to protect fragile ecosystems and induce recycling. Rebelling against pristine newness and patent commercialism, these individuals express personal attitudes which may contradict current tides of fashion.

Architect Lebbeus Woods, describing his proposals for war-torn Sarajevo, in *A+U*, a Japanese architecture and urban design journal, stated, "Now, there is no choice but to invent something new which nevertheless must begin with the damaged old, a new that neither mimics what has been lost, nor forgets the losing, a new that begins today, in the moment of the loss's most acute self-reflection." Clearly, that kind of new is the direction being pursued by New Modern mavericks.

above Sleek table and floor lamps designed by Dieter and Quint are on display around their Williamsburg, Brooklyn, loft studio and residence. The metal chair was designed by Dieter.
photo Carla Breeze

JAMES DIETER & LESLIE B. QUINT

The New York City-based designers James Dieter and Leslie B. Quint are graduates of the Rhode Island School of Design. Quint obtained a B.F.A. in jewelry and light metals; Dieter a B.F.A. in industrial design. Both have been honored with awards for their work, which currently is focused on the production of a line of residential lighting fixtures.

In addition to his work with Quint, Dieter designs furniture and interiors that express the clash between sleekly machined products and the handmade. His rough, yet elegant, furnishings appear somewhat crude, but are, in fact, painterly constructions with allusions to the gestural moment.

In the loft studio space where the two work and Dieter resides, disjunctive remnants from street *arte povera* collide with the lamps the pair have designed, as well as furniture by Dieter. The strength of the space is its quality of randomness.

above In the sleeping area of the Dieter/Quint loft, the bedside table holds two of the designers' simple, yet sculptural, lamps, which explore the shadow and patterning potential of light.
photo Carla Breeze

left Floor lamps suggest dressmakers' forms.
photo Carla Breeze

right Ackerman and Mullaney's loft
has evolved from a raw, industrial
space into a habitable gallery-style
residence. In the portion of the
loft used as a study hang examples
of Ackerman's early assemblage
paintings.
photo Carla Breeze

below The loft's furnishings, like the
cherry wood Shaker-style bed in
the loft's sleeping room, were
chosen for their simple, clean
design, which works well against
the pure white walls.
photo Carla Breeze

ANDREA ACKERMAN &
TOM MULLANEY

Contrasts abound and are exploited in the
loft space shared by artists Andrea
Ackerman and Tom Mullaney. Existing
period details in the fairly raw New York
City loft have been retained and serve to
enhance the effect of the installation-scale
projects the artists produce which are
incorporated into their home and work
space.

Mullaney is a painter and sculptor with
an M.F.A from the School of the Museum
of Fine Arts, Boston, who exhibited at one
time with Boston's Stux Gallery. He
describes the process of creating a habitable space as, "both intentional and unin-
tentional, a ruin that became stabilized to
preserve and enhance a general flow of air
and abundant light.

Ackerman, who attended Yale and
obtained her doctorate in medicine at
Harvard, believes that the loft space has
affected her work. One piece in particular,
titled Change of State, is representative of
"the transformation from monocular
Cartesian perspective to a neo-Baroque
visual order. This conception of space,
which embraces both complexity and con-
tinuity, forms a variety of solutions to the

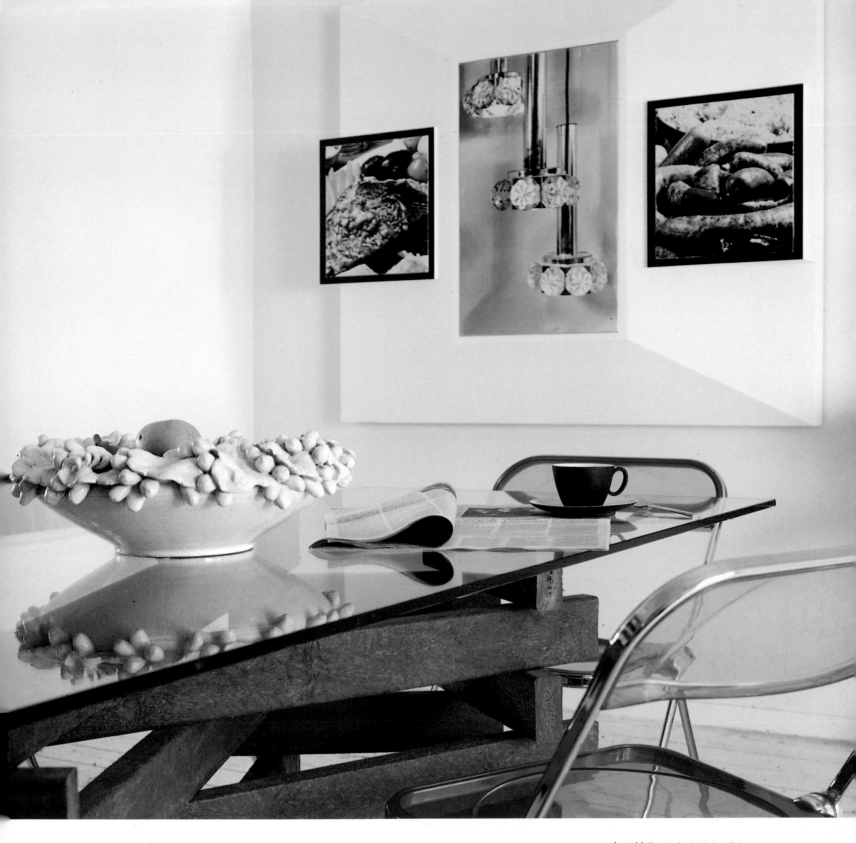

challenges of deconstructionist/postmodern architecture. It is relevant in an increasingly complexly connected culture, still bounded by the ultimate point of reference, the human body and mind."

above Mullaney devised the dining room table, by stacking recycled plastic "redwood" to form a base for the glass top, actually a glass door salvaged from a gallery. The tinted lucite chairs were designed in the late 1960s by Giancarlo Piretti. The photographic sculpture is an example of Mullaney's work. *photo* Carla Breeze

above The Blackburn/Reed loft is filled with personally meaningful items, and is organized into areas that flow into one another. The painting is one of Reed's early efforts.
photo Carla Breeze

JEAN BLACKBURN & JASON REED

Inspired by questions concerning boundaries, how space is defined, and strategies for understanding the world, artists Jean Blackburn and Jason Reed have created a mutated loft home for themselves in the rescued Greenpoint section of Brooklyn. Blackburn, who received an M.F.A. from Yale and teaches at the Rhode Island School of Design, sees her work and environment as incorporating "grids, sorting, and compartmentalization for comparison, building mental constructs from physical 'stuff.' " She says, "We tend to surround ourselves with objects that are reassuring, familiar, and known.... However, experience, cultural change, illness, forgetting, chaos, and mistakes all work to undermine these created boundaries and definitions. They are constantly in flux. Ideas leak into each other. Edges blur...."

Blackburn and Reed have embellished the space in their own fashion, reflective of their shared sensibility, with familiar and somewhat disparate objects. However, they retained many of the modifications created by a former tenant and existing industrial details, such as the wrapped bands of utility pipes around the length of the space that form a kind of factory-style wainscoting. Their loft is a reconstruction, an architectural collage of their personalities, and of the "history" of the space itself.

above Blackburn and Reed are interested in form for form's sake, and have not altered many of the rough-edged elements of the loft space, such as a fire-escape doorway, appreciated for its grittiness, juxtaposed against more conventional furnishings in the living space.
photo Carla Breeze

left A candelabra sculpture by Blackburn, in the sleeping area of the loft, exemplifies her interest in "subverting the mundane object's reassuring definitions by reconfiguring them."
photo Carla Breeze

below left Under the windows in the sitting area, radiator pipes appear as a kind of industrial-style wainscoting. The mismatched furniture and objects in the loft are collected by Blackburn and Reed for their striking forms, that when placed adjacent to one another become even more interesting.
photo Carla Breeze

below The Baxter loft successfully examines the interaction of angled elements, the effect of light, and the juxtaposition of rich and untreated materials. Steel and sandblasted glass doors separate the loft's study/guest room from the second-floor landing
photo Carla Breeze

opposite A maple shelf juts out from the stairway base on the lower level. Breslin, who worked in Isozaki's Tokyo office for a year, shares with the Japanese master a taste for incorporating bold sculptural elements to enrich the interior experience.
photo Carla Breeze

LYNNE BRESLIN

The three-floor loft space atop a former warehouse in Manhattan's TriBeCa had been remodeled into a residential space prior to architect Lynne Breslin's involvement in the project. Breslin articulated and brought power to the interior by imposing a "skewed ellipse...as a central organizing device, which at once defined, but also energized, the space." She also enclosed and incorporated the loft's existing bathrooms, closets, and utility spaces with a three-story canted and expanding box that can be "followed as it moves through space."

Exquisite attention to building processes and to the conflicts inherent in creating "public" and "private" space have been demonstrated in Breslin's residential work as well as in exhibitions she's designed for many institutions, including the Whitney Museum, the United States Holocaust memorial Museum, and the Brooklyn Botanical Gardens. The concept of home as a repository of memory is explored in the physical design of her installation at the Holocaust Museum, with material construction symbolized by lathe walls. In a section of a Thomas Hart Benton exhibition she created at the Nelson-Atkins

Museum in Kansas City, Missouri, Breslin worked with the idea of voyeurism: "In the middle of the room is an area I call the Venetian blind room—it's a surface you can see through but not be seen."

That concept is also apparent within the Baxter loft. The definitions of exterior and interior are subverted. Interior windows provide vistas through the space, which can be closed off or left open.

Breslin obtained her M.Arch degree from Princeton University. A Luce Scholarship allowed her to spend a year working in the Tokyo atelier of the renowned master of spatial effects, Arata Isozaki. She has the ability to create a particular sense of place and use materials in an inventive, yet harmonious, way.

above & left Slick and rough surfaces and materials are combined to create a powerfully seductive effect in the Baxter residence. *photo* Carla Breeze

background Plan, Baxter loft. *drawing* Courtesy of Lynne Breslin

above The stairway that winds its
way through the Baxter loft culmi-
nates in the approach to the roof
deck. Light catches the uneven
finish of the stair rails.
photo Carla Breeze

left A bedroom is placed behind an elliptical wall, pierced by an interior window.
photo Carla Breeze

below Breslin harmoniously "plays" with angles and creates framed views throughout the Baxter residence.
photo Carla Breeze

right Two apartments on the Upper West Side of Manhattan were merged into one by Billinkoff. The extra space enabled the architect to create an entire "wing" for the client's children and their au pair. The space's envelope is contemporary, with floating ceiling elements and few molding details, but Billinkoff has chosen floral fabrics and sturdy traditional furnishings to soften the geometry.
photo Carla Breeze

DONALD BILLINKOFF

Floral patterns and rich colors are integrated delightfully with generic materials and sumptuous granites, marbles, and historical details in architect Donald Billinkoff's work. In using evocative materials and textures and applying them to contemporary architectural forms, he produces environments that are at once both traditional and utterly modern, serious and whimsical. Close collaboration with his clients produces spaces that contain references to older architectural themes, but are clearly modern in spatial organization and spirit. Layers of elements—patterns, wooden slats, and soffits—overlay the original interiors in his residential projects, intertwining figures and forms, old and new components.

For a Greenwich Village brownstone project, Billinkoff collapsed and expanded space. The interior boundaries now are permeable, and the rear garden space bursts upon the formal first floor, while maintaining the building's original sense of enclosure.

"Organized for the needs of a young family in which both adults have professional careers, the house is organized around the typical brownstone's vertical and horizontal circulation paths," he says. "Throughout development of the residence, this essential nature was preserved."

The town house is arranged to provide spaces for both family activities and privacy. A "parents-only" floor features small studies and bathrooms for each spouse, as well as their bedroom. A two-story atrium connects the lower two floors, enlivening the family space with natural light and views into the luxuriant garden.

In Billinkoff's renovation of an apartment on Manhattan's Upper West Side, he inserted new walls into the shell of the existing space to create juxtaposed layers of "new and old." Clerestory windows and low walls expand intimate rooms. The original structural elements of the ceiling float independent of the floor plan below. Layers of color and wall textures visually separate the surfaces, while at the same time fuse all the elements into a unified scheme. Abundant natural wood brings warmth and richness to the space.

Before opening his own practice, Billinkoff was an associate architect with Hardy Holzman Pfeiffer Associates.

right Elegant birch cabinets and granite counters make the kitchen space in the Upper West Side project functional and beautiful.
photo Carla Breeze

below right Chintz wallpaper lends coziness to the more formal, contemporary fittings in the kitchen of a Greenwich Village town house made over by Billinkoff.
photo Carla Breeze

above Architectural features of the renovated Greenwich Village town house, such as arched openings, moldings, fireplace surrounds, and the general placement of windows have been retained, though the interior has been opened up considerably to light and the outdoors. *photo* Carla Breeze

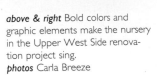

above & right Bold colors and
graphic elements make the nursery
in the Upper West Side renovation project sing.
photos Carla Breeze

far right Billinkoff outfitted a child's
playroom in the large Upper West
Side residence with an "urban tree
house." The floral wallpaper invig-
orates the space.
photo Carla Breeze

above Natural motifs bring the garden inside throughout Billinkoff's Greenwich Village project.
photo Donald Billinkoff

left Ultra-contemporary furniture contrasts with original Victorian-era detailing in the living room.
photo Carla Breeze

below Furnishings selected for the living area project create an eclectic mien, with both traditional and contemporary associations.
photo Carla Breeze

STEVEN HOLL

Refined. Artful. Intense. Evocative. Modern. These words describe the creative, concentrated spaces created by architect Steven Holl. His work has a quiet power, with forms, colors, and materials combined and interacting to create a sense of place.

Holl's often austere interiors seem to convey an inner quest for meaning in architecture. He plays, in very serious fashion, with ideas of open and closed space, of interior "landscapes" that require the individual to conform to them. Practicality is not the overriding issue. Holl is concerned more with the "essence" of a building, "transcending physical and functional requirements," as he has written in *Anchoring*, a monograph on his work published by the Princeton Architectural Press.

above Within a pristinely detailed residence in Fukuoka City, Japan, Holl explores the relationship between open and closed space, using hinged wooden panels as the means for transformation.
photo Matsuo Photo Atelier

right A number of surface effects, forms, and materials are incorporated into flats within Holl's Hybrid Building in Seaside, Florida.
photo Paul Warchol

opposite Holl's embellishments to the interiors of the Hybrid Building's multi-level flats bring a poetic quality to the spare architecture.
photo Paul Warchol

below The living room of a Gramercy Park apartment contains a floating box that conceals video equipment amid a wall of bookshelves. Geometric layering effects, a la Mondrian, are seen throughout the project.
photo Carla Breeze

opposite In the same residence, two-toned wooden doors with frosted-glass inserts enclose the dining space and are rendered in a style that is complementary to the design of the contemporary built-in buffet.
photo Carla Breeze

SUSANA TORRE

Chairman of the Architecture and Design Program at Parsons School of Design architect Susana Torre was asked by clients to design their new apartment when they relocated to New York City. Their previous residence, in Cincinnati, was a Victorian house, with three floors and plenty of space for their children. Now grown, the children are no longer the primary design consideration.

The clients, however, have their own needs. They have a large library, which needed to be accommodated. They wanted to furnish the new abode with as much furniture passed down through their families as possible. Addressing these and several other design issues, Torre created an interior that could be modified for various purposes, employing frosted-glass screens to enclose spaces as desired. Bookshelves line the entry and living room, with built-in furnishings carrying through the black and brown color scheme—perhaps Torre's response to the view of the Romanesque revival-style building across Gramercy Park from the apartment.

NEW MODERNS

below Henner Kuckuck's
Stockholm Chair employs traditional furniture materials in method
akin to the Japanese art of origami.
photo Dan Nelken

opposite The beauty of decay,
an appreciation for time's effect
on a space, is presented in the
"restoration" of Brooklyn's Majestic
Theater, a project executed by the
Hardy Holzman Pfeiffer firm.
photo Durston Saylor

Subversions of form and materials, inversions of conventional interior and exterior structures and contexts, and potent transformations of vernacular elements are the basis of a new kind of architecture and design practice—a new take on Modernism. Asymmetrical trusses, patterned brick, floral wallpapers, cantilevers, and corrugated steel—intrepid elements and parodies of the past are mingled with utilitarian and industrial substances. Post-industrial amenities converge with Modernism's historical compost. The sterile "machine for living" has been banished by a new generation of designers and architects who feel comfortable with the past, yet are enthusiastic about Space Age materials, industrially produced generic elements, environmental protection, popular culture, even kitsch.

The work of early 20th-century architects, who had a formative influence on the development of early Modernist style, such as Adolf Loos, Peter Behrens, and Jose Plecnik, is being reconsidered by today's practitioners. New Modernists are not solely nostalgic or revivalist, however. They are not mere parodists, with overly obvious references tacked on to their buildings and interiors. Instead, the emerging generation is concerned with the establishment of a distinct point of view that is comfortable with the past, and not as dogmatic as we now consider traditional Modernism to be.

New Modernists are also environmentally aware, building within the urban landscape, recycling buildings, exploring old and new materials, employing historic elements. When designing new structures outside of the urban context, they allow existing organic features to shape their forms, melding them to the earth for aesthetic as well as for practical reasons.

Oriented to comfort, both visual and visceral, while employing contemporary methods and materials, the architects and designers who are categorized as New Modernists produce work that can be called compassionate, humane. This humanism, however, coalesces with ever-present technology, with strikingly effective, and often refreshing, results. New Modern has liberated architecture from the doctrinaire, and the impact these architects and designers are making will redirect the course of residential design in the future.

right In renovating a Greenwich Village residence, Berke restored the interior architecture, retaining original moldings where possible, but keeping things simple and pristine, making the spaces non-competitive with the client's collection of Arts & Crafts furniture. *photo* Carla Breeze

DEBORAH BERKE

Morality and social conscience were inseparable from aesthetics for early Modernists. Adolf Loos's incendiary tirade against the Secessionists, *Ornament und Verbrechen* (Ornament and Crime), published in 1908, suggested his passionate adherence to a code of design ethics by its title alone. Loos argued that materials, in and of themselves, should offer whatever embellishment necessary for a design. His projects, such as the Muller villa in Prague, illustrate his point clearly. Loos's use of sensuous travertine, wood paneling, and finely finished fabrics, verifies his passion for exquisite materials and workmanship, allowing them, rather than superficial applied ornament, to create the "decorative" statement. He believed that the power of form and the organic quality of natural materials unmodified by "fussy" interaction were enough.

Architect Deborah Berke, who holds a B.Arch from the Rhode Island School of Design, and a Master of Urban Planning degree from City University of New York, executes work that has an austerity comparable to Loos's, yet employs her own vocabulary. "I believe in an architecture of restraint," says Berke.

above The kitchen and adjoining
breakfast room in the Greenwich
Village project are tranquilly spare.
Windows are left undressed—
there is no place for superfluous
details.
photo Carla Breeze

left Some features original to the apartment have been maintained.
photo Carla Breeze

below left A traditionally rendered pantry hall connects the apartment's kitchen and formal dining room.
photo Carla Breeze

opposite The bedroom wall in Iacucci's West Midtown loft/studio is pierced by square and rectangular openings. A bedside table is constructed in a fashion reminiscent of the work of Gerrit Reitveld.
photo Carla Breeze

background In an elevation of a Berlin building project Iacucci is involved with, geometric forms are stacked to create a striking overall pattern.
drawing Courtesy of Paola Iacucci

PAOLA IACUCCI

Architect Paola Iacucci, whose paintings and projects over the past few years can be seen as poetic metaphors and visions of urban space, has perfectly reflected this ethos in her New York City studio—an imperfect mirror with gilding and scuffs that document use and utility. From her windows overlooking Manhattan's West Side, Iacucci gathers the strands of the landscape into her arms to reform the image of urbanism. Concretely aware of the social, political, economic, and engineering factors that shaped the view from her studio, she demonstrates the positivism espoused by Le Corbusier (though his attitude was eroded by his fear of contamination of the non-Modern).

In the studio, the fetish for finish has been rejected. Iacucci prefers the expressive qualities of commonplace surfaces and raw materials. Plywood is used for its laminated edges; dry wall construction is economical, but also easily manipulated, and is left untreated. Rawness and the unfinished, almost casual approach does not preclude any lack of purpose. Iacucci accepts the nature of use, weathering, and the effect of time, a metaphor for the human body, scarred with birthmarks and continually moving through and toward life and death crises, which mar the body but do not deny its ultimate beauty.

Slivers of light lead one through to the arc defining the foyer of the space. The walls of rooms concerned with the stuff of living—sleeping, cooking—contain rectangular apertures and include attached or built-in furnishings that remind one, according to Kenneth Frampton, writing about Iacucci's work in *Domus* in 1992, "of the work of Gerrit Rietveld and of Pierre Chareau's Maison de Verre, although in neither instance can we speak of direct quotation."

Iacucci taught at the Politecnico in Milan prior to coming to the United States, where she teaches at Columbia University and the University of Pennsylvania. She maintains studios in Milan and New York City.

above A sliver in the wall between the bedroom and dining area of Iaccuci's loft allows for the transmission of light, as well as creates intriguing vistas for occupants of both spaces, confounding the conception of public versus private space.
photo Carla Breeze

left Iacucci has deliberately left the surfaces of the drywall partitions in her loft rough and messily unfinished, to counter the idea of "perfect" space, and to give texture to the environment.
photo Carla Breeze

above & right Living and working areas merge in Iacucci's loft. The walls she has added, to enclose "private" bedroom spaces, stop short of the ceiling, to maintain the pattern of the beams and a sense of openness.
photos Carla Breeze

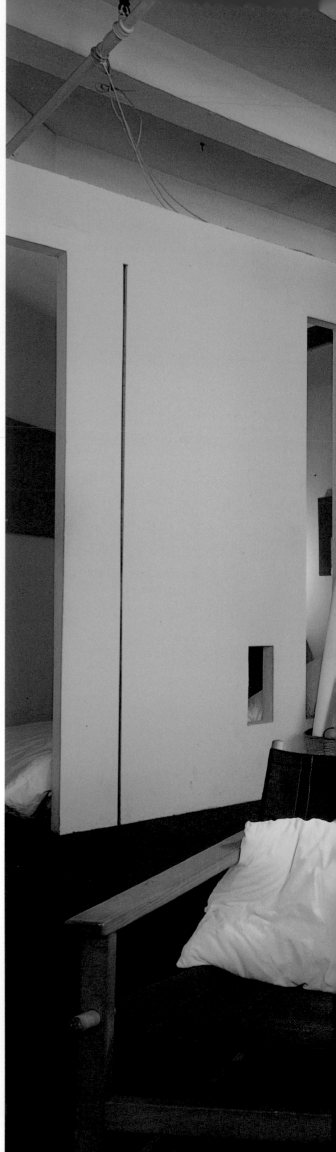

above The Reflected Farmhouse complex is composed of new and restored structures that relate to one another, creating the impression of permanence.
photo Carla Breeze

right The grain silo structure surrounding the lap pool is clad with rough timber elements created from tree trunks that had to be removed during construction.
photo Carla Breeze

opposite In a space connecting the living room to a breezeway, Gluck uses exterior stonework to bring the outdoors inside.
photo Carla Breeze

PETER L. GLUCK

Collapsing space, folding volumes, and re-assembling solid structures in ways that create the illusion of flight, Peter Gluck grasps the essential nature of permeable boundaries in architecture. Allusions to the Modern technology of the curtain wall and a building's skin are seen in Gluck's dynamic buildings, in which he "pushes the envelope," so to speak.

Gluck's work is rational, yet ambiguous; elements parody the very foundation of meaning and content through form. Balance and harmony are subject to re-evaluation. Fragments disrupt the correct-ness. Working with modules evocative of perfection—squares, cubes, spheres, and other "pure" geometric forms—Gluck inverts and subverts logic, juxtaposing the "real" and the reflected, transparency with volume, often in a fashion that can be read as ironic. Gluck uses concrete, stucco, and other materials to create what could be termed a "nondimension."

opposite Gluck paraphrases historic architectural models with the asymmetrical truss support above the main living/dining/kitchen space of the Reflected Farmhouse.
photo Carla Breeze

left Antique furniture is "fused" into the overall contemporary and colorful interiors of the Reflected Farmhouse, as in this niche corner of the master bedroom.
photo Carla Breeze

below In the master bath, Gluck has skillfully combined elements of the sleek variety with more organic, natural materials.
photo Carla Breeze

background Floor plan, Reflected Farmhouse.
drawing Courtesy of Peter L. Gluck & Partners

right Lattice work along the street level of Kunihiro's Kinuta, Japan, residence is installed to provide privacy, and does not block the clear vistas toward Mount Fuji from the second and third levels of the house.
photo Shinkenchikusha

background Isometric, Floating Tea House installation, New York City.
drawing Courtesy of George Kunihiro Architect

opposite The south elevation of the Kinuta house accommodates an open space created by sliding the main volumes past one another. The view of the surrounding suburban fabric is blocked out by the concrete wall.
photo Shinkenchikusha

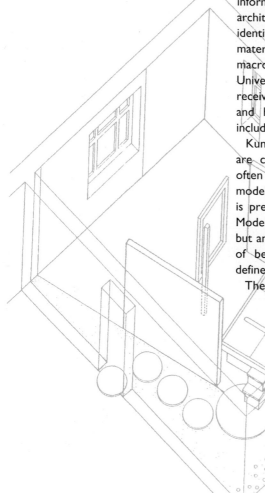

GEORGE KUNIHIRO

Eastern and Western design philosophies inform the work of New York City-based architect George Kunihiro. He attempts to identify the "essence" of a building, its materiality in relation to its details—the macro and the micro. Trained at the University of California, Berkeley, Kunihiro received an M.Arch degree from Harvard, and has taught at several institutions, including Harvard, Yale, and Columbia.

Kunihiro creates simple structures that are complex in detail, site-specific, and often restrained versions of historical models. An underlying sense of practicality is present as well. There is a minimalist Modern outlook inherent within his work, but an appreciation for traditional notions of beauty make his work less rigidly defined.

The design of Kinuta house, says Kunihiro, "is derived from the site, an incline, and a view of Mount Fuji in the distance. By maximizing the quality of the site, we sought to create a three-dimensional exterior space within the restricted site, and to employ the concept of *shakkei* (borrowed scenery) to amplify the perception of open space in and around the house. The parti consists of two rectangular volumes, in shear, tied together by a central linear circulation core. By sliding the main volumes past each other, we were able to create a three-story open space on the south elevation and the parking space on the north side of the structure. From the base of the vertical open space, a piece of nature in the form of the sky is juxtaposed with the open latticework of the wooden deck above, to create a quiet courtyard for the study on this level."

left & above Kunihiro's Floating Tea House, designed as a temporary installation at New York City's Elysium Arts gallery, offers a dramatically serene and fully contemporary environment, using minimal elements—a reference to the elegant simplicity of the Japanese tea ceremony itself. *photos* Shinkenchikusha

CLASSICISM

opposite The Villa Viare, a residence designed by Alexander Gorlin, updates the Mediterranean-revival tradition. A "romantic" pergola leads to the main door of the house.
photo Steven Brooke

below A classic image from the Sistine Chapel is printed on plastic material, folded and secured with grommets to make the Poster Stool, designed by Henner Kuckuck.
photo Dan Nelken

With its order and harmony, Classicism has an eternal appeal, especially during periods of chaos and social and economic upheaval. Cultural memory is instantly evoked by overt Classical references. Abstracted and muscular formalism, strong, simple geometry imposes a structure that is as reassuring as rational. The order signified, however, may be illusionary in contemporary buildings and interiors.

Various architects and designers in the late 20th century have burned out on the pervasive sterility represented in works by iconic Modernists like Walter Gropius, Le Corbusier, and Ludwig Mies van der Rohe. They instead look to Athens, Rome, or Florence for inspiration, but do not forget the "progress" of the centuries in between. Classical references, as the new millennium evolves, may act in some designers' work as a critique of the coldness of the curtain wall. Ornament is not seen as crime by some. Others embrace only Classical forms, without the intrusion of decorative "whimsy."

The new Classicism announces the flow of past into present, no longer separated by distinct boundaries of time or space—two elements of 20th-century modernity which have become collapsed and telescoped with instant access to imagery and place via electronic and mechanical means. Pediments and cornices, quoins and keystones, affirm a conservative instinct among these practitioners, but the new Classicism is not purely retro. The

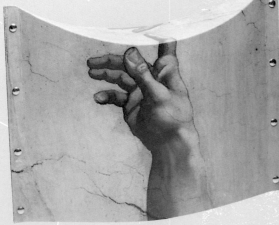

forms may be familiar, but can be handled in astonishingly new ways. Inherent are the infrastructure developments of the past one hundred or so years—indoor plumbing, electricity, heating, air-conditioning. Old forms may sheath the fabled and fully realized "machine for living," reflective of the dichotomy that pervades post-industrial life.

right The entrance foyer of Gorlin's Villa Viare has a stripped-down appearance, with gentle reminders of historical precedents, such as columns, baroque lighting fixtures, and some molded details that one would expect in a villa-style structure.
photo Steven Brooke

below Elevation of the grand, but not grandiose, Villa Viare.
drawing Courtesy of Alexander Gorlin

ALEXANDER GORLIN

A graduate of Cooper Union's School of Architecture, with an M.Arch degree from Yale, Alexander Gorlin works in a studio near Manhattan's Cooper Square, lined at ceiling cornice level with models for his historicist residential projects. A former recipient of a Rome Prize, which allowed him to study architecture and design in the Eternal City, Gorlin manipulates the Classical vocabulary with élan.

For Gorlin, Italian villas and palaces inspire his stylistic references, though they are presented in an entirely modern idiom. Columns, pediments, and cornices are essential parts of his architectural speech, and are used for evocative purposes, in conjunction with slick modern surfaces. Many of Gorlin's country house designs are reminiscent of Andrea Palladio's villas, though his sensibility and handling of details makes them clearly contemporary and not derivative by any means.

above & left In the Villa Viare living room, arched windows top French doors that open to a courtyard, the walls are painted in a style reminiscent of a palazzo, dark-stained wood beams cross the ceiling, and there are sheer, yet abundant curtains installed— all clearly romantic touches that link the interior with the past. Gorlin isn't creating a pure period piece, however. He has adopted historic elements, incorporating them "comfortably" into what reads as a wholly contemporary environment.
photo Steven Brooke

right The recently installed pool on the grounds of Villa Viare is reached via a grand stairway structure constructed to present an authentic Italian atmosphere on American shores.
photo Steven Brooke

below The walls in the Villa Viare dining room are topped with an elaborate frieze molding depicting cherubs.
photo Steven Brooke

below Nowell applied industrial-grade roofing copper as a back-splash in the kitchen of Lewis's Newton, Massachusetts, basement loft space for a textural, patterned effect. Through the opening in the wall, with traditional molding at its base, is an example of the artist's intricate Neoclassical-style sculpture work.
photo Carla Breeze

right Interior walls in the space create a "cityscape" impression within the rather low-ceilinged space. A pediment, with a school-type clock amusingly placed at its center, is positioned atop the kitchen area.
photo Carla Breeze

ROBERT LEWIS & GREGORY NOWELL

Numerology, shrouded figures, and broken columns inhabit the dark visions of sculptor Robert Lewis, who worked closely with architect Gregory Nowell on the conversion of a basement-level space in a former school building into his and Laura Duffy's residence and studio. Nowell, an M.Arch graduate of the Massachusetts Institute of Technology, devised a plan that worked well within the difficult space. He designated the lower basement level as a studio, with raised levels for living, bedroom, kitchen, and dining areas.

Nowell planned the space as an armature for Lewis, whose sculpture has progressed to the realm of rooms; the pieces are almost Neoclassical installations. Within the studio-residence, Lewis, inspired by Palladio's delicate and luscious Teatro Olimpico in Vicenza, has embellished every corner creating a stage-set-like setting. Theatrical effects, including false façades, an artificially illuminated oculus, and the simulation of sunlight pouring through backlit louvers, add further drama to the interiors. The artist's own sculpture pieces have become an integral part of the arrangement, each spotlighted on a tiny stage.

left Art produced by Lewis was taken into consideration in the design of his residence and studio.
photo Carla Breeze

far left The basement space has few windows and low ceilings in certain areas. A wall almost touches the ceiling support beam in this "room," and separates it without closing it off entirely.
photo Carla Breeze

below The added architectural elements in the Lewis loft are free-standing, with the basement envelope left apparent on the ceiling.
photo Carla Breeze

PETER L. GLUCK

Purchased by art collectors Lawrence and Linda Levine, Eastward represents a collection in its own right: a main house, a theater, and various smaller guest houses interspersed around the Fairfield, Connecticut, property. The compound was originally built by an owner rumored to have been a French set designer. Thus, the early 20th-century American Craftsman period buildings at Eastward are cast with a French Provincial flair.

Architect Peter Gluck worked with the Levines to modify several parts of the complex. He was sensitive to the original context presented in each structure, though creating thoroughly contemporary environments. The romantic nature of the Arts & Crafts period atmosphere has been respected and stabilized where possible. In instances where a complete gut was required, Gluck has not turned his back on historical references, making allusions to the old in the new.

above & right Eastward is a complex of buildings in Fairfield, Connecticut, renovated by Peter Gluck. The half-timbered exterior of the circa 1912 buildings, including the theater structure shown, have been restored, but not tampered with.
photo Carla Breeze

above Atop the raised bed platform in the master bedroom in the main house, Gluck has incorporated a stepped ceiling drop, a subtle allusion to a traditional medieval bed canopy.
photo Carla Breeze

above Tradition reigns in the library of Eastward's main house, decorated by professional interior designer Paul Egee, who worked with Gluck in creating a cohesive relationship between architecture and furnishings.
photo Carla Breeze

left In the Eastward kitchen, separated from the entrance foyer by a streamlined wooden wall partition, the original period millwork, door, and windows have been restored, with no new architectural flourishes hindering their impact.
photo Carla Breeze

above The romantic effect of the
exterior of Eastward's numerous
buildings was maintained in the
restoration.
photo Carla Breeze

right Modified and modernized,
the Eastward kitchen offers many
new elements that Gluck had
built specifically to preserve the
craftsman-era aesthetic.
photo Carla Breeze

right An appropriately French-accented look is imparted through the selected furnishings and decorative elements Rosen has installed in the main room of Lanesend's library/guest house pavilion.
photo Carla Breeze

below The dining room of the traditionally styled Greenwich, Connecticut, residence is formally attired, harking back to another era and way of life.
photo Carla Breeze

JILL MANES ROSEN

Lanesend was built in rural Connecticut during the height of American fascination with French Provincial and English Tudor styles. Charming and imaginative houses, like Lanesend, often categorized under the heading Wall Street Pastoral, built during the first 40 years of the 20th century, integrated American-style conveniences within romantic, picturesque trappings.

In renovating Lanesend, designer Jill Manes Rosen wanted to maintain the property's French Provincial atmosphere. Her concept was "to use various historical references in a unique way rather than replicating a particular past." In fact, even though there is a heavy French accent, via antiques and wall surfaces, the house could exist nowhere else—a double-car garage is attached to the property.

right & below right The rural European flavor of Lanesend's architecture is heightened by appropriate landscaping that looks as if it has been there for years. Only a television antenna hints that this is a dwelling of 20th-century vintage.
photos Carla Breeze

above Rosen's scheme for the
Lanesend drawing room is quite
regal, and has both English- and
French-style antecedents.
photo Carla Breeze

below, opposite, & background The "Professor's Study" studio in Charlottesville, Virginia, designed by Dunham-Jones and LeBlanc, is a classic composition in the minimal Modernist mode, concerned with issues of symmetry and balance.
photos Phillip Jones
drawing Courtesy of Ellen Dunham-Jones & Jude LeBlanc

ELLEN DUNHAM-JONES & JUDE LeBLANC

Ellen Dunham-Jones obtained her M.Arch degree from Princeton in 1993 and, in addition to her practice with Jude LeBlanc, teaches at the Massachusetts Institute of Technology. Dunham-Jones and LeBlanc Architects has merited awards for several projects, and the firm's work has appeared in numerous journals, as well as 18 Houses, *published in 1992 by the Princeton Architectural Press.*

In their Charlottesville Studio project, the architects have been influenced by vernacular and Classical architecture. The studio's stripped-down appearance and simple, logical construction is related to precedents set in the past. It is also planned to fit in with the context: "Like its neighbors, [it] combines masonry and balloon-frame construction," says Dunham-Jones. Though new, it is not a shocking addition to the Charlottesville landscape.

above A balance is created
between the curved wall and
linoleum floor pattern and the
placement of fixtures in the
bathroom.
photo Phillip Jones

opposite The studio's library space
is cleanly symmetrical.
photo Phillip Jones

HAMPTONS STYLE

below A Searstyle chaise longue designed by Constantin Boym features store-bought elements, such as pillows that tie to the frame, creating a more elegant expression than the presumed original aim of the Sears products.
photo Courtesy of Constantin Boym

opposite For "C" Pool in the Hamptons, George Ranalli uses interlocking asymmetrical frets to produce a visually exciting outdoor space.
photo Carla Breeze

While many New Modern architects and designers are constrained to work only in dense urban areas, the opportunity to explore new forms has traditionally been offered by commissions in places like the Hamptons, the once rural region of Eastern Long Island now dotted with the weekend and summer retreats of wealthy New Yorkers. Seaside, Fire Island, Cape Cod, the islands of Martha's Vineyard and Nantucket, and other residential enclaves where second and vacation houses are built, are filled with cutting-edge architectural expressions, probably because of the willingness of clients to experiment when the residence is not their primary abode.

Stylistically, the work of architects and designers in the Hamptons and other "laboratory-for-design" communities is quite varied, with nods to local traditions incorporated in some instances; a clean, vacuum-like slate for others. The Hamptons accommodate not only formal villas, where entertainment occurs on a grand scale, but small-scale projects like cottages and pool houses. There is also the opportunity to become more involved with the placement of a building within a programmed landscape—creating a new context, in a sense—and the construction of ancillary structures, such as pavilions for swimming pools, guest accommodations, outdoor living venues, gardens, grottoes, even follies, which can address any number of stylistic tendencies.

The clean palette of a rural or exurban site frees the architect or designer from the limits of the urban grid. Formal investigations are possible that challenge traditional notions of what a living space is, and how we live in such spaces. Architectural rules are as relaxed as the intended atmosphere within such Hamptons-style projects.

background Elevations of "C" Pool pool house.
drawings Courtesy of George Ranalli, Architect

right The dynamic shape of the pool is designed to accommodate various types of water activity.
photo Carla Breeze

below Perimeter walls, required for safety and security, are pierced to allow views into the surrounding wooded area.
photo Carla Breeze

GEORGE RANALLI

Architect George Ranalli designed "C" Pool in collaboration with his clients for their Hamptons residence. A pool house is scheduled to be built in 1996. Providing seclusion and maintaining the wooded quality of the landscape, Ranalli positioned a fence around the perimeter of the pool space, pierced with narrow openings that permit views of the surrounding natural environment.

"C" Pool was designed to fulfill exacting criteria from the client related to various recreational functions. The lap lane was to be no more than 4-feet deep, to enhance a novice swimmer's perception of competency in water of any depth. A step runs along the length of the shallow end of the pool as a place for children to safely splash. A "swim out" was added to the deep end to facilitate swimmers' exits from the pool.

top At "C" Pool, traditional wood is used for the fencing, with copper caps and rivets protecting vertical elements.
photo Carla Breeze

left A whirlpool tub is housed in a separate raised structure.
photo Carla Breeze

opposite Employing glass and glazed tiles, Ranalli adds color to "C" Pool.
photo Carla Breeze

background Plan, "C" Pool.
drawing Courtesy of George Ranalli, Architect

right Gwathmey/Siegel's de Menil residence re-invents the concept of the Hamptons seaside villa. *photo* Norman McGrath

below The pool area attached to the de Menil house is raised to allow for spectacular views up and down the Long Island shoreline. *photo* Norman McGrath

GWATHMEY/SIEGEL

Magnificent summer residences, large enough to accommodate formal functions and weekend house parties, as well as a retinue of service workers, have traditionally dotted the shoreline of the Hamptons. The de Menil residence, in Amagansett, New York, designed by the Manhattan firm Gwathmey/Siegel, recalls this era of grand structures, but in a New Modern, rather than a shingled, vein.

Charles Gwathmey obtained his M.Arch degree from Yale, while Robert Siegel earned his M.Arch at Harvard. Their evocative building style employs vernacular materials within a sophisticated context.

above The interiors of the de Menil residence are furnished with classic 20th-century pieces, a contrast to the slickly Modern envelope.
photo Norman McGrath

right The arrangement of spaces within the villa is quite complex, with multiple façade overlays, interior windows and structures, circulation bridges, and skylighted ceiling sections. A greenhouse area lies within the perimeter of a glazed exterior wall.
photo Norman McGrath

left & below Like traditional Hamptons villas, the de Menil residence is clad in wood siding that weathers to a silvery gray tone, though it is applied to a complexly New Modernist structure.
photos Norman McGrath

above A classically upscale, resort-style look was devised for a pool house designed by Gorlin for the Hamptons property of fashion designer Adrienne Vittadini. *photo* Ed Addeo

ALEXANDER GORLIN

Since Renaissance times, an aspect of city living in Italy has been the retreat into the country, explained as the urban sophisticate's sentimental nostalgia for a simpler, rural lifestyle. Italian villas were often working farms with elegant homes for city-based owners set amid formal gardens.

Alexander Gorlin has explored the concept of the contemporary Italianate villa in Villa Cielo, a country house located in Westchester County, New York. Like Palladio, the Renaissance Mannerist architect, Gorlin employs low horizontal forms, placing the house on a hillside overlooking the lush landscape below. At Villa Cielo and in other resort-oriented projects, Gorlin applies the harmonies of Classicism to a thoroughly modern structure, producing a soothing, comfortable, and ultimately simple effect.

left Columns define the porch area of the Vittadini pool house, framing the view of the swimming pool and the pastoral landscape beyond.
photo Ed Addeo

bottom left The shingle-clad, columned pool house is in keeping with the architecture of the main Vittadini residence.
photo Ed Addeo

above Perched atop a hill overlooking the rolling countryside, Villa
Cielo is a stripped-down version of
a Palladian country house.
photo Ed Addeo

above Villa Cielo's comfortably furnished octagonal living room features plate-glass versions of classic window configurations. The windows are untreated to allow for clear views out over the landscape.
photo Ed Addeo

left The classic forms of an Italian country house are reinterpreted by Gorlin at Villa Cielo in New York's Westchester County.
photo Ed Addeo

above The thoroughly modern entrance to the Fischl studio has a monumental air, with flanking stone piers. The oversized door glazing and the smaller, typically New England-size window exemplify Skolnick's manipulation of scale throughout the project.
photo Courtesy of Lee Skolnick

right Skolnick designed an enclosed breezeway access to Gornick's studio, employing the language of New England vernacular-style porches to merge the old and new.
photo Courtesy of Lee Skolnick

below A new studio was created within the footprint of an old barn at the Hamptons compound Skolnick designed for artists Eric Fischl and April Gornick.
photo Courtesy of Lee Skolnick

LEE SKOLNICK

With much of his work concentrated on the South Fork of Long Island, otherwise known as the Hamptons, architect Lee Skolnick, when working on projects in that area, or receiving commissions in other locales, maintains an aesthetic that is appropriate to the context. His choices of forms and materials are dictated by site, the area's history, and a playful eye.

Whether the houses he designs are from scratch or renovations and expansions of an older property, Skolnick addresses traditional as well as fully contemporary notions, creating a coherent relationship between exterior and interior, blending the slick and the mundane, and fulfilling the needs of the individual residents. The architect is especially popular with artists, who see the Hamptons as a bucolic refuge from the intensity of Manhattan, and who enlist Skolnick to convert old farmhouses and outbuildings into germane settings for living and working.

left The walls on the second floor of the Gomick/Fischl house were removed to create a spacious master bedroom, dressing area, and a bath space, with a suspended sink, treated sculpturally. Fischl collaborated with Skolnick on the design of the sink area.
photo Durston Saylor

below Skolnick worked with his artist-clients to maintain an austerity of form and detail appropriate to a rural farmhouse. In the living room, wainscoting covers the walls. A formal composition is created by the positioning of square windows on either side of the bluestone hearth.
photo Durston Saylor

above In a Greenwich, Connecticut,
residence by Skolnick, each space,
such as the master bathroom
shown, contains intimate vistas.
photo Mick Hales

above Spaces such as this multi-level hallway are the result of the organic placement of Skolnick's Greenwich, Connecticut, house on its meandering, curved, sloped site.
photo Mick Hales

left A loft, or interior treehouse, is provided in each child's room of the Greenwich project.
photo Mick Hales

above A Bridgehampton, New York, residence designed by Voorsanger & Mills is composed of three linked pavilions, clad in Hamptons-style shingles. Bedrooms are located in side wings, with the central shared living space in the central pavilion.
photo Courtesy of Voorsanger & Mills

opposite A sense of openness is achieved in the Bridgehampton house. Unadorned walls are pierced to create interesting patterns.
photo Courtesy of Voorsanger & Mills

below The placement of the house on a slope allows for soaring ceiling heights and dual-level spaces inside that belie the single-story front façade.
photo Courtesy of Voorsanger & Mills

background Isometric, Bridgehampton residence.
drawing Courtesy of Voorsanger & Mills

VOORSANGER & MILLS

Architects Bartholomew Voorsanger and Edward Mills, who formed a partnership in the 1980s, produced a number of residential and commercial projects considered to be innovative and influential. Some of their works are referred to as masterpieces within the postmodern genre.

In the 1990s, the architects have pursued separate interests. Mills heads up a solo practice. Voorsanger, who graduated from Harvard with an M.Arch degree in 1964, has combined a solo practice with commitments to the American Institute of Architects (he is a past president), and is currently the chairman of the Buell Center for Architecture at Columbia University and chairman of the Port Authority of New York and New Jersey's review board.

A Bridgehampton, New York, residence designed by the pair was conceived as a modern version of the type of shingled farmhouse found throughout the Hamptons. The clients, two brothers, required a central shared area with two master suites, one at either end of the house. Utilizing traditional balloon framing and shingle cladding, the house is arranged in three pavilions. The central structure houses the entrance and shared living and kitchen spaces. Built atop a slope, the residence is composed of two "bands," with the lower band hunkering down into the slope to accommodate the living room and a swimming pool.

above Berke & McWhorter's vernacular-style Schmidt house is on a brick-paved road within the planned, low-scale, new community of Seaside, along the Florida coast, meant to be a "perfect" incarnation of a beach town, and the site of several experimental-type forays by New Modern architects and designers.
photo Steven Brooke

right A wonderful rooftop gazebo for outdoor dining and entertaining crowns Berke & McWhorter's Averett residence at Seaside.
photo Steven Brooke

opposite The Schmidt residence in Seaside, Florida, designed by Berke & McWhorter is simple and airy, with numerous windows and doors providing for optimum ventilation. Dunes and foliage have been left intact or planted back to retain the spirit of the place.
photo Steven Brooke

BERKE & McWHORTER

Located on the Gulf of Mexico, Seaside, Florida, is a planned community, which has become a chic venue for the display of work by contemporary architects. Alexander Gorlin, Steven Holl, and Deborah Berke in partnership with Carey McWhorter are among the high-profile architects designing houses and other types of buildings at this beachside resort. Berke and McWhorter have reassessed and reconfigured vernacular-style frame construction house types to create simple, referential retreats at Seaside.

BIBLIOGRAPHY

Stanley Abercrombie, "Italy: The First Built Parts Of a Cemetery Famous Before Building Began," *Architecture*, August, 1983.

Theodor W. Adorno, *Prisims*, Cambridge: The MIT Press, 1990, 5th Printing.

Editorial Staff, "EcoAlert: Pallet-able Design," *Architecture*, January, 1992.

Diana Agrest, *Design from Without: Theoretical Framings for a Critical Practice*, Cambridge: The MIT Press, 1991.

Stevens Anderson, "A Place to Discover Art: Arthur Roger Gallery, New Orleans," *Architecture*, October, 1989.

Steven M.L. Aronson, "Portrait of the Artists," *Architectural Digest*, April, 1989.

Gaston Bachelard, *The Poetics of Space*, Boston: Beacon Press, 1994.

Reyner Banham, *Design By Choice*, New York: Rizzoli, 1981.

Reyner Banham, *Theory and Design in the First Machine Age*, Cambridge: The MIT Press, 1980.

Marisa Bartolucci, "The Seeds of a Green Architecture," *Metropolis*, April, 1992.

Russell A. Berman, *Modern Culture and Critical Theory: Art, Politics, and the Legacy of the Frankfurt School*, Madison: University of Wisconsin Press, 1989.

Thomas Bernhard, *Correction*, Chicago: University of Chicago Press, 1979.

Aaron Betsky, *Violated Perfection: Architecture and the Fragmentation of the Modern*, New York: Rizzoli, 1990.

Minor Bishop, "American Architectural Fashion," Unpublished Manuscript (with comments by Vincent Scully), 1952.

Peter Blake, *The Master Builders*, New York: W.W. Norton, 1960.

Rosemarie Haag Bletter, "Kahn and His Defense," *Design Quarterly*, Number 59.

Harold Bloom, Editor, *Romanticism and Consciousness*, New York: W.W. Norton, 1970.

Murray Bookchin, *Toward an Ecological Society*, Montréal: Black Rose Books, 1986.

Daniel J. Boorstin, *The Americans*, New York: Random House, 1965.

Lynne Breslin, "Vacant Lots Project," *Progressive Architecture*, January, 1990.

Geoffrey Broadbent, Richard Bunt and Charles Jencks, *Signs, Symbols and Architecture*, New York: John Wiley & Sons, 1980.

Patricia Leigh Brown, "Allegory or Your Money Back," *The New York Times*, February 13, 1992, Section C.

Susan Buck-Morss, *The Dialectics of Seeing: Walter Benjamin and the Arcades Project*, Cambridge: The MIT Press, 1991.

Akiko Busch, "As American as Apple Pie," *Metropolis*, March, 1992.

Matei Calinescu, *Five Faces of Modernity: Modernism, Avant-Garde, Decadence, Kitsch, Postmodernism*, Durham: Duke University Press, 1987.

Robert Campbell, "Artytecture: What Young Designers Do When There's Nothing to Build," *The Boston Globe Magazine*, December 5, 1993.

Gilles Deleuze, *The Fold: Leibniz and the Baroque*, Minneapolis: University of Minnesota Press, 1993.

Deborah K. Dietsch, "Green Realities," *Architecture*, June, 1993.

Ellen Dunham-Jones, "Of Type and Thing," *18 Houses*, Jude LeBlanc, Ed., New York: Princeton Architectural Press, 1992.

Ellen Dunham-Jones and Jude LeBlanc, "Alchemical Transformation: Building Into Architecture," *OZ*, Volume 13, 1991.

James Marston Fitch, *American Building: The Historical Forces That Shaped It*, New York: Schocken, Second Edition, 1973.

Hal Foster, editor, *The Anti-Aesthetic: Essays on Postmodern Culture*, Port Townsend: Bay Press, 1983.

Hal Foster, editor, *Vision and Visuality*, Seattle: Bay Press, 1988.

Kenneth Frampton, *Modern Architecture: A Critical History*, New York: Oxford University Press, 1980.

Kenneth Frampton, "Paola Iacucci e Laura Briggs, Appartamento a Manhatthan," *Domus*, June 1992.

Mario Gandelsonas, "The Modern Villa between Abstraction and Representation," *GA*, January, 1984.

Margot Gayle and David W. Look, *Metals in America's Historic Buildings*, Washington, D.C.: U.S. Department of the Interior, National Park Service Cultural Resources, 1992.

Victoria Geibel, "The Stillness of Space," *Metropolis*, January/February, 1988.

Brendan Gill, "Improving on Tradition in Connecticut," *Architectural Digest*, September, 1992.

Joseph Giovannini, "Arata Isozaki: From Japan, A New Wave of International Architects," *The New York Times Magazine*, August 17, 1986.

Brad Gooch, "The New Bohemia," *New York*, June 22, 1992.

Adam Goodheart, "Artificial Greenery," *Design Quarterly*, Fall, 1992.

Charles Gwathmey and Robert Siegel, "deMenil Residence," *GA*, January, 1984.

Steven Holt, "Three for the Way We'll Be," *Metropolitan Home*, January, 1991.

Hardy Holzman Pfeiffer Associates, *Hardy Holzman Pfeiffer Associates: Buildings and Projects, 1967-1992*, New York: Rizzoli, 1992.

Dolores Hayden, *Redesigning the American Dream: The Future of Housing, Work and Family Life*, New York: W.W. Norton, 1986.

Robert L. Herbert, editor, *Modern Artists On Art: Ten Unabridged Essays*, Englewood Cliffs: Prentice-Hall, Inc., 1964.

Andreas Huyssen, *After the Great Divide*, Bloomington & Indianapolis: Indiana University Press, 1986.

Paola Iacucci, "Architecture and the City: Berlin Spandau Wasserstadt," 1992.

Paola Iacucci, "Didactic in Silence," January, 1994

"The 38th Annual Design Review," *I.D.*, July/August, 1992.

Julie Iovine, "Downtown Split-level," *Metropolitan Home*, October, 1990.

Robert Janjigian, *High Touch: The New Materialism in Design*, New York: E.P. Dutton, 1988.

Charles Jencks, *Modern Movements in Architecture*, New York: Doubleday Anchor Press, 1973.

Eve M. Kahn, "Hardy Holzman Pfeiffer Associates Take On a Tradtional Interior," *Traditional Building*, January/February, 1994.

Stephen Kern, *The Culture of Time and Space 1890-1918*, Cambridge: Harvard University Press, 1983.

John A. Kouwenhoven, *Half a Truth Is Better Than None*, Chicago: University of Chicago Press, 1992.

Heidi Landecker, "In Nature's Arms," *Architecture*, June, 1993.

Le Corbusier & Ozenfant, "Purism," reprinted in *Modern Artists on Art: Ten Unabridged Essays*, edited by Robert L. Herbert, Englewood Cliffs: Prentice-Hall, 1964.

Laurene Leon, Artist's Statement, August, 1994.

Frank Lupo, "Statement," 1994.

Ellen Lupton, *Mechanical Brides: Women and Machines From Home to Office*, New York: Princeton Architectural Press, 1993.

Donlyn Lyndon and Charles W. Moore, "Images That Motivate," *Places*, Volume 9, Number 1, Winter, 1994.

Machado and Silvetti Associates, "New House on the Block," *Architectural Record*, April, 1994.

Ross Miller, "Interview: George Ranalli," *A+U*, August, 1990.

William Mitchell, "The Electric Agora," *ANY*, November/December, 1993.

Francesco Moschini, "Paola Iacucci: Other Buildings," *Three Houses and Other Buildings*, Milan: Gangemi Editore, 1991.

Mohsen Mostfavi and David Leatherbarrow, *On Weathering: The Life of Buildings In Time*, Cambridge: MIT Press, 1993.

Peter Murray, *Architecture of the Italian Renaissance*, New York: Schoken, 1984.

Herbert Muschamp, "If You Squint, This Is Not a Faulty Tower," *The New York Times*, August 21, 1994.

Editors, "Painting by Numbers: The Search for a People's Art," *The Nation*, March 14, 1994.

Gregory Nowell, *Close to the Edge: Finding the Hammerhead Bar*, Unpublished Manuscript, 1989, 149.

Claes Oldenberg, *Proposed Monuments and Buildings: 1965-69*, Toronto: Ryerson Press, 1969.

Alberto Pérez-Gomez, *Architecture and the Crisis of Modern Science*, Cambridge: The MIT Press, 1983.

Charlotte Perkins Gilman, *Herland*, New York: Pantheon, 1979 Edition.

Richard Pommer, "Structures for Imagination," *Art In America*, March/April, 1978.

George Ranalli, "Getting a Handle," *DESIGN Quarterly*, Spring, 1992.

Amos Rapoport, *House Form and Culture*, Englewood Cliffs: Prentice-Hall, 1969.

Patricia Reiter and Wellington Reiter, "Just a White Box," *Art New England*, June/July, 1993.

Beverly Russell, *Elle Decor*, July, 1994.

Saskia Sassen, *The Global City: New York, London, Tokyo*, New York: Princeton University Press, 1991.

Vincent Scully, "A Virtual Landmark," *Progressive Architecture*, September, 1993.

Alison Sky and Michelle Stone, *On Site 5/6 On Energy*, New York: SITE, Inc., 1974.

Jorge Silvetti and Rodolfo Machado, "Villa on Lake Pergusa," *Progressive Architecture*, January, 1985.

Citation: Architectural Design: Jorge Silvetti, Vacation House, Djerba, Tunisia, *Progressive Architecture*, January, 1978.

Architectural Design Award, Machado and Silvetti, "Villa on Lake Pergusa," *Progressive Architecture*, January, 1985.

Suzanne Slesin and Michael Steinberg, "Hamptons Style," *Architectural Record*, April, 1990.

Katherine Cole Stevenson, *Houses by Mail*, Washington, D.C.. Preservation Press, 1988.

Manfredo Tafuri, *The Sphere and the Labyrinth: Avant-Gardes and Architecture from Piranesi to the 1970's*, Cambridge: The MIT Press, 1990.

John Thackara, "Design as Cultural Engineering," *Axis*, Volume 46, Winter, 1993.

Calvin Tomkins, *Off The Wall: The Art World of Our Time*, New York: Doubleday, 1980.

Lauretta Vinciarelli, "Red Rooms, Water Enclosures and Other Unfolding Spaces," Lecture, Princeton University, School of Architecture, March 31, 1993.

Richard Vine, "Feminine Devices," *Art In America*, December, 1993.

Marcus Whiffen, *American Architecture Since 1780: A Guide to the Styles*, Cambridge: MIT Press, 1981.

James Wines, *De-Architecture*, New York: Rizzoli International, 1987.

Stuart Wrede, "*Complexity and Contradiction* Twenty-five Years Later: An Interview with Robert Venturi," *American Art of the 1960s*, New York: The Museum of Modern Art, 1991.

Tetsuro Yoshida, *The Japanese House and Garden*, New York: Frederick A. Praeger, 1958.

APPENDIX

Andrea Ackerman
Tom Mullaney
152 Broadway
Williamsburg, New York 11211
(718) 384-1208

Alfredo De Vido
David Cook
Alfredo De Vido Associates
1044 Madison Avenue
New York, New York 10021
(212) 517-6100

Cornelius M. Alig
10 West Market Street, Suite 700
Indianapolis, Indiana 46204
(317) 464-8214

Deborah Berke
Carey McWhorter
Berke & McWhorter
270 Lafayette Street
New York, New York 10012
(212) 219-2088

Donald Billinkoff
139 West 82nd Street
New York, New York 10024
(212) 496-7772

Minor Bishop
150 East 37th Street
New York, New York 10016
(212) 685-5095 or (516) 671-3015

Jean Blackburn
Jason Reed
164 East 9th Street
Brooklyn, New York 11211
(718) 388-4946

Constantin Boym
Laurene Leon
56 West 11th Street
New York, New York 10014
(212) 674-8508

Lynne Breslin
210 Riverside Drive
New York, New York 10025
(212) 864-7976

James Dieter
Leslie Quint
5 Diamond Lamps
235 Grand Street
Brooklyn, New York 11211
(718) 384-6887

Laura Duffy
Robert Lewis
447 Lowell Avenue
Newtonville, Massachusetts 02160

Ellen Dunham-Jones
Jude LeBlanc
Dunham-Jones & LeBlanc
81 Bellmont Street
Somerville, Massachusetts 02143

Frank Lupo
Dan Rowen
Mary Evelyn Stockton
Frank Lupo & Dan Rowen Architects
448 West 37th Street, #12B
New York, New York 10018
(212) 947-9109

George Kunihiro
George Kunihiro Architects
121 West 27th Street, #1004
New York, New York 10016
(212) 463-8727

Andra Georges
685 West End Avenue, #16B
New York, New York 10003
(212) 222-1205 or (212) 787-7800

Peter L. Gluck
19 Union Square West
New York, New York 10025
(212) 255-1876

Alexander Gorlin
380 Lafayette Street
New York, New York 10003
(212) 228-9000

Charles Gwathmey
Robert Siegel
Gwathmey/Siegel
475 10th Avenue
New York, New York 10001
(212) 947-1240

Hardy Holzman Pfeiffer Associates
902 Broadway, 19th Floor
New York, New York 10010
(212) 677-6030

Idi Henderikse
Jan Henderikse
119 Hall Street
Brooklyn, New York 11205
(718) 638-1592

Steven Holl
435 Hudson Street
New York, New York 10001
(212) 989-0918

Paola Iacucci
448 West 37th Street, #8C
New York, New York 10018
(212) 629-3083

Henner Kuckuck
11-55 45th Avenue
Long Island City, New York 11101
(718) 392-6444

Giuseppe Lignano
Ada Tolla
Lot/Ek
55 Little 12th Street
New York, New York 10014
(212) 255-9326 or (718) 488-8955

Rodolfo Machado
Jorge Silvetti
Machado and Silvetti
560 Harrison Avenue
Boston, Massachusetts 02118
(617) 426-7070

Elizabeth A. McGee
Mark S. Pecker
526 10th Street
Brooklyn, New York 11215
(718) 768-1130

Edward I. Mills
50 White Street
New York, New York 10013
(212) 334-9891

Charles R. Myer
875 Main Street
Cambridge, Massachusetts 02139
(617) 876-9062

John Myer
School of Architecture and Planning
MIT
265 Massachusetts Avenue, Room N51-332
Cambridge, Massachusetts 02139

Gregory Nowell
487 Washington Street
Brookline, Massachusetts 02146
(617) 232-0964

George Ranalli
150 West 28th Street
New York, New York 10001
(212) 255-6263

Patricia Reiter
Wellington Reiter
Reiter & Reiter
449 Lowell Avenue, #11
Newton, Massachusetts 02160

Jill Manes Rosen
45 Buckfield Lane
Greenwich, Connecticut 06831
(203) 869-4370

Lee H. Skolnick
7 West 22nd Street
New York, New York 10011
(212) 989-2624

Susana Torre
14 East 4th Street
New York, New York 10003
(212) 228-3573 or (212) 229-8955

Steven Izenour
Denise Scott Brown
Robert Venturi
Venturi, Scott Brown & Associates
4326 Main Street
Philadelphia, Pennsylvania 19127
(617) 426-3604

Lauretta Vinciarelli
137 Greene Street
New York, New York 10012
(212) 254-0986

INDEX

ACKNOWLEDGMENTS

I gratefully acknowledge the following individuals: Barbara Rosen, Reference Librarian, University of New Mexico Zimmerman Library; Wayne Decker; Paola Iacucci; Lauretta Vinciarelli; Andrea Ackerman; Merle O'Keefe; Diana I. Argrest; and Minor Bishop. All of these individuals devoted time and consideration to the project, and together we explored the concepts and issues raised by the project.

Penny Sibal, Managing Director, Susan Kapsis, Managing Editor, and Francine Hornberger, Assistant Editor at PBC International enthusiastically supported this project and I am indebted to them for their valuable contributions. Richard Liu, Technical Director, was a superb resource whose technical direction facilitated a fresh approach for the design of this book.

All of the architects and designers also contributed to this effort, and of course, without them, there would be no New Modern.